How to Be Ageless

Growing Better, Not Just Older!

❧

SUZY ALLEGRA

CELESTIALARTS

Berkeley • Toronto

CELESTIALARTS
P.O. Box 7123
Berkeley, California 94707
www.tenspeed.com

A Heart & Star Book

Distributed in Australia by Simon and Schuster Australia, in Canada by Ten Speed Press Canada, in New Zealand by Southern Publishers Group, in South Africa by Real Books, in Southeast Asia by Berkeley Books, and in the United Kingdom and Europe by Airlift Book Company.

Cover and text design by Margaret Copeland based on a design by Deborah Jones
Cover artwork by Suzy Allegra

Library of Congress Cataloging-in-Publication Data is on file with the publisher.

Printed in the United States of America
First printing this edition, 2002

1 2 3 4 5 6 7 8 9 10 — 05 04 03 02 01

Acknowledgments

It takes a village to raise children . . . and in this case, it took more than a village to birth this book. There are so many people who have contributed to this book—some directly and some simply by their contributions to my life. Therefore, it would probably take another book to thank everyone who added their support and wisdom in indirect ways. But I will at least begin with the following.

First, I am eternally grateful to my family . . . to my parents, Betty Gallagher (bless her soul) and William Froug, who gave me the gift of my birth, love and lessons that have shaped my life and constant support of my creativity. To my stepfather, George Gallagher, who was more like a father than he can imagine, for his steady assistance, and to my stepmother, Chris Michaels, for being more like a sister than she can imagine.

My siblings and their families have all been wonderful cheer-leaders—Nancy Earth; Lisa, Brad, and Ashley Hirano; and Jonathan, Chie, Andrew, and Emily Froug. I am especially grateful to Jonathan for always being there—as a sounding board, best friend, and reality-checker.

I have been blessed with many mentors throughout my life and I am grateful to all of them. There are four who stand out, however, and have been there with me on this journey of learning the lessons of agelessness. First of all, a huge "thank you" to Teresa Von Braun, my spiritual mentor, teacher, and counselor for helping me find my path and stay on it. I also greatly appreciate the support and guidance given to me by Susan RoAne, best-selling author; Sarah Reeves-Victory, well-known communications expert; and Randy Gage, master marketer and copywriter.

There are so many friends who have been there for me in a myriad of ways over the years that it would take several pages to mention them all. There are three, however, that I must mention individually. One, Barbara Cox, has been a stalwart advocate for almost 30 (!) years, since we were roommates in college. I am deeply appreciative for her loving support. The two others have helped more recently in significant ways—by giving me friendship, advice, and assistance, and by kicking me in the pants when needed. Thank you, Bob Casanova and Rick Bowers, for your care and help.

I also want to thank Marisa Taylor, my friend and ex-first-grade student, who introduced me to the concept of being "ageless" when we traveled together in Europe a few years ago. As we talked about the issues of aging, she told me that she felt ageless (at age 27). I realized that this was exactly what I was aiming toward too.

I know I could never have gotten to this point without the help of dozens of health-care practitioners who have allowed me to move through all the resistance that showed up in my body. I thank you all for help via EMDR work, acupuncture, cranial sacral, and other bodywork. I know that each of us is one whole being—body, mind, emotions, and spirit—that work in one realm always helps in the others.

Lastly, I can't thank enough my wonderful editor—Tim Polk. Of course, I couldn't have completed this without him. But my appreciation goes further than that. His editing is the best kind that one can have—making my words read better, but at the same time letting my voice still come through. Thank you for your editing wisdom.

Table of Contents

Welcome the Wisdom and Gifts of Aging

Foreword

How to Be Ageless, Growing Better, Not Just Older! is a helpful book with the purpose of inspiring and directing us to face the present and future with a positive attitude. Suzy Allegra has drawn upon her experiences to provide us with an excellent understanding of what it means to be Ageless.

Throughout the book, major emphasis is placed on denouncing the theory that "youth is king." The author makes clear her belief that in order to be Ageless we must first change our mindset from a youth-focused attitude to a successfully aging attitude. Older persons are challenged in this book to acknowledge reality, embrace their creativity, and enjoy their remaining years.

Gerontologists today recognize that in order to age successfully, we must first accept and embrace the fact that we are aging. We must focus on the positive aspects of the aging process. This book helps bring those positive aspects to light.

I am so happy to see an author take charge in denouncing current misperceptions about aging. I relish every opportunity we have to impress upon people of all ages that changing times require changing attitudes. In reading this book, it is easy to see that the author is ahead of the game in acknowledging this fact.

The author also provides us with insightful exercises and helpful strategies that allow us to focus on areas of our lives requiring a change in attitude.

Readers who are able to take the material in this book and put it into practice will be on their way to aging successfully. This book comes at an opportune time to spread the word to persons of all ages that focusing on trying to look younger only buys into the false "youth is king" theory.

It would be a benefit to readers of all ages to read and live this book.

Melinda Ares, M.S.
Gerontologist

What Does "Ageless" Mean Anyway?

&

We live in a youth-obsessed society. Everywhere we see the "youth is king" concept promoting everything from cars, soap, and cigarettes to music, clothing, and cell-phones. Everything old is disregarded or discarded. We treat our older citizens the same way, too. As an aging baby boomer, I not only don't want to be disregarded or discarded, I don't want to see it happen to anyone else.

Why? I believe that, as elders, we have many gifts to give others—gifts of wisdom that come from the vast experiences we've had along our life's path. I also believe, perhaps because of our penchant for youthfulness, that most people are afraid of aging (and, dying). They do everything they can to resist aging, and consequently contribute to the problem.

It hasn't always been this way. Long ago before the industrial revolution (and in indigenous cultures today), elders were and are revered and honored for their knowledge. We must go back to honoring the elders in our society if we are going to age successfully with joy, vitality, and grace because it is important to feel valued for our contributions. Feeling valued gives us a sense of contentment and peace of mind. *If we are able to first value and honor ourselves, we will then be able to change how others perceive us.* This is where agelessness comes in.

To be ageless, as I use the word, is to feel the worth of ourselves in a timeless manner—not considering how old (or young) we are. It means disregarding the features and noticing the benefits. That may be sales talk, but it fits for the importance of honoring the wisdom of those with experience. Don't let wrinkles, graying hair, or double chins (the features) get in the way of valuing the gifts that you have to offer. Be proud of your knowledge, insight, and know-how (the benefits). These are what count most in the world—not your face or body.

But we, as a culture, have bought into the fable that our physical features matter most. I spent much of my life there—even though I knew it shouldn't be that way. It's hard to fight against millions of dollars of advertising that shouts, "Youth is king!" Now is the time to change all of that. It's time to stand up and be proud of all that we have to offer and start living life the way we want to, not the way Madison Avenue tells us to. That's what being ageless means to me…honoring the enduring and endearing qualities that we all have, no matter how old or young we may be. It means letting those timeless aspects of ourselves shine through no matter what our exteriors present.

The dictionary defines ageless as "seemingly not aging, eternal." And that's the quality that I believe we all have *internally*. It is not about our physical attributes—it's about our mental, emotional, and spiritual ingredients. Aren't these what *truly* matter most? Do you love your family or friends because they have thick or curly hair, a stunning smile, or taut skin? I'd like to think not. And somewhere deep inside, don't you believe they love you for your internal beauty—your conscience, compassion, and caring? *That's* your agelessness.

It's challenging, I know. In order for the eternal traits to radiate, there needs to be an understanding of yourself at the deepest level. In part, it means acceptance of what is going on at any moment in your life. This is different than being resigned, which has an underlying emotion of resentment. Acceptance means valuing what life has given you. We don't have to like it, but we can realize that there is something for us to learn or appreciate from the present circumstance. Agelessness also involves elements of gratitude, peace of mind, and trust.

For example, I get migraine headaches. They are extremely painful and I don't like them. But when I get them, I realize there are reasons why I am ill. Some of these reasons might be physical and some are mental or emotional. I accept that I am having a migraine and work to discover what caused it so that I can make some positive change to avoid, postpone, or lessen the severity of another one. I need to stay away from perfume, not work for a company where I am angered by their policies, and give myself more time to rest. I know that I may still get migraines even if I do take care of myself in these ways, but I also know that I am continually finding greater peace of mind because I am taking responsibility for making positive changes in my life. I find that when I continue to make these positive changes, my migraines occur less often and are less severe. I am grateful for all the good in my life, even when I have times of pain. This, to me, is living life to the fullest—regardless of my age or stage in life. It's being ageless.

Believe in your agelessness, accept that life isn't the same with each passing year, *yet, know that you can still be vital*. Learn to have gratitude for what you have had in the past and for each moment you have now. Give up the notion that "youth is king." Don't buy into the ads that promote youthfulness as the outcome of purchasing any product or service.

At the same time, tell yourself the truth. That means being completely honest about your motives for doing what you do. In other words, are you using face creams (or working out, etc.) to help you maintain your skin and body so that you are the best you can be at your age, or are you trying to look and *be younger* than you are? The pain comes when we tell ourselves one thing (that we're doing this to feel our best), but when the real truth is something else (that we do want to *be* younger). The way to feel joy and peace as you age is to acknowledge reality and to accept the inevitability of aging. Accepting your aging gracefully and with an ageless quality means trusting the process of life. It also means being able to honor your body as it is now and being okay with taking longer to recover from physical exertion or not exerting yourself as strongly as you did in the past. When you start to feel ageless, you realize that it doesn't matter if you take longer to recover because it is your timeless qualities inside you that count!

To reach a sense of being ageless also means to acknowledge the emotions of change and loss. Feeling the emotions that come as you learn to accept who you are now allows you to let go of the old images of how you were as a younger person. It is great to have fond memories, but when they stop you from accepting who you are now, they get in the way of feeling the peace of mind that is a part of successfully aging. Making a commitment to yourself to go through this process allows you to become the wise elder that you are inside already. It is a significant step to being ageless.

Give yourself the kudos you deserve—for your wisdom and your accomplishments. Too many elders have bought the cultural story that they aren't worth much and, therefore, don't feel good about themselves and what they have to offer the world. Feeling good about yourself is at the foundation of feeling ageless.

Lastly, your attitude means *everything* in being ageless. There has been much research on the importance of a positive attitude on healing more quickly. A positive attitude has also been shown to be one of the most important characteristics necessary for longevity. Enjoy your golden years by noticing the wonder of life around you and by staying lovingly connected to family, friends, and/or pets. When you are able to welcome the gifts of aging, you will be able to feel ageless. And as you are embracing your life's path, aging with joy, vitality, and grace, you will be giving a contribution to future generations as well—the gift of knowing that they, too, will be able to be honored and recognized for their worth. A timeless gift from an ageless person!

I know—understanding these concepts is simple, but living them is quite a different story. That's why I've written this book: both to introduce you to the concept of ageless living and to show you—in specific terms and ways—how to do so.

How to Use this Book

❧

Though there is a particular order to this book that made sense to me, it is important that you use the book in a way that works best for you. You can read all of it or you can first jump right into the middle or end and read any chapter that seems significant to you. This may be a guidebook, but *let yourself be the guide*—which, in this case, means to trust your instinct or intuition. If some of the subject matter doesn't fit with your experience or beliefs, don't let that stop you from discovering information in other chapters. I believe that when we pick up a book and are drawn to it, for whatever reason, we will learn at least one or two meaningful things. Let this book give you the support you deserve to be able to enjoy your life's path so that you will be able to feel the wonder of being ageless.

Give Up the Idea
that "Youth is King"

❧

ONE

Believe in Yourself

~

In order to give up the "youth is king" belief, you must first believe in yourself. This means having a high degree of self-confidence. It is believing in your worth as a fine human being. You don't need to be the best at anything to feel good about yourself. If you are a kind and caring person, that is good enough. If you are unable to believe in your self-worth, you will find difficulty in asserting yourself and standing up for what you believe is right, honest, and fair. You won't be able to stand up to our cultural attitude toward elders.

I must admit, I have gone back and forth believing in myself over my fifty plus years. As I was turning 50, I began believing in myself, and my ability to speak up in my personal relationships, better than I had ever done before. A few weeks before I turned 50, I started expressing myself in ways I had never

> *"Believe that life is worth living and your belief will help create the fact."*
> —William James

done before. It was exhilarating! I had long ago been able to be assertive in relationships that were not close, but now I had stepped up to a new level of assertion in deeper relationships as well. My feelings of confidence were immense. My happiness increased because I was now taking care of myself by speaking up about what wasn't working for me. I knew something could be done to work out the difficulties because I was finally talking about my needs.

However, shortly after turning 50, I found some of this confidence waning. This was about my physical being. Though I started noticing wrinkles years earlier, they didn't bother me then. But after 50, I not only noticed the wrinkles, I noticed the sagging skin on my arms and the sinewy lines on my neck. I started to feel less attractive. Yet, some months after that, after relatively innocuous encounters with two strangers, I realized that it isn't my wrinkling skin but an attitude of aliveness, openness, and caring that keeps me attractive. In two separate instances, I was complimented and told how beautiful I was by a man and a woman young enough to be my children. I realized they weren't talking about my looks. They were noticing my smile and my warmth. These two people helped me remember my previous confidence. To relearn that youth (and external beauty) is not king (or queen!) was beneficial to me because, otherwise, I could have continued to lose my belief in myself.

Believing in yourself means believing in your good, not in whether or not you are youthfully slim, youthfully attractive, or youthfully sexy. Rather, it's more about believing in your inner worth . . . your warmth and your caring for others. While self-esteem is never stagnant—it waxes and wanes on a minute-by-minute basis—if you have a solid foundation of self-worth, you can go through the highs and lows of feeling good or not-so-good about yourself *knowing* that you really are a good person whether or not you're having a "bad hair" day.

As we are growing up, we somehow learn to believe that it is only the youthful ones who get jobs, who succeed in love and life. The truth is that there is often a great deal of pain in youth. There are so many fears that teenagers and young adults have: What am I going to do with my life? Am I going to succeed? Get married? Have children? Live near or far?

Those questions, while they may never go away completely, seem less important as we age. If we do some deep soul-searching, we begin to know that we can survive, that life isn't perfect or happy ever after, and that we can enjoy ourselves no matter what our age. We know that, even if we are aging, we can still have good jobs, good relationships, and good fun.

Believing in Yourself Exercise:

- Do you believe in yourself? Do you have confidence in who you are? Think about and/or write examples to support your view. Too many people I know say, "Oh yes, I have confidence. I believe in myself." But when I watch their actions, hear their words, they show the deeper truth— one that is the opposite of what they say.
- Do you believe that you have something important to contribute to this world no matter what your age? This doesn't have to be a major contribution, like discovering the cure for cancer. It means any effort—to help a child grow, to give support and friendship to others, to create team spirit at work.
- Do you believe your beauty (worth) is more than skin deep? This is a true test of whether or not you have given up the notion that youth is king.

Strategies to Jump-start Solutions:

- If you have come to the honest conclusion that you don't have the confidence that will help you to grow in an ageless manner, it's time to do some soul-searching. There are a variety of ways and methods to do this. Before doing any of the following, however, I suggest that you do this simple but difficult exercise: (a) Call 10 of your closest friends and family members—more is even better. Ask them to tell you over the phone (while you write) or have them write down and send, fax, or email you 10 or more words that describe your positive characteristics, and (b) Read these lists twice daily, morning and night. This is difficult because most people who don't have self-confidence can't bear to hear good things about themselves.

After working with yourself in this way, you can also continue working with your confidence in these ways:

- Learning about and using daily affirmations (also called cognitive behavioral therapy) and visualizations (mental rehearsal),
- Reading self-help books and attending seminars, and
- Working with a therapist, coach, or clergyperson and/or with groups that support personal growth.
- If you feel like you do not have anything to offer the world, do the exercise above and ask your friends and family what you have given them or others or have contributed to the world. Then go to the library and sign up to teach reading to someone who can't, or volunteer for a nonprofit organization that matches your areas of interest.

"We grow neither better nor worse as we get old, but more like ourselves."
—May Lamberton Becker

- If you cannot get beyond believing that beauty is only skin deep, read about and look at photos of some elders who have believed in themselves. Some recommendations: Grandma Moses, Jimmy Carter, Mother Teresa. When you look at their photos, look at their eyes. Can you see the sparkle that moves beyond any wrinkles that appear? Look at the peace in their expressions. Their beauty goes beyond their looks.

Final Thoughts

Without confidence and a belief in yourself, your aging will continue to plague you. Even plastic surgery won't eliminate the inner stress that belies your lack of confidence. Begin now to notice how much you've given to your family, friends, and community. Remember that your beauty is deep within your eyes, in who you are, and what you've given to others. It's not just skin deep.

"The most exhausting thing in life is being insecure."
—Anne Morrow Lindbergh

TWO

Tell the Truth

❧

As we age, it's sometimes hard to tell ourselves the truth. Sometimes we tell ourselves we're really doing something (e.g., using cosmetics, getting a face-lift, pumping iron) because we want to be the best-looking 50- or 60-year-old that we can be. But the truth is we really want to be younger than we are; we aren't accepting our age.

Sometimes we look in the mirror and say we are fat, ugly, and stupid when we're not. I did this for much of my life. It was finally in my mid-thirties that I was able to believe in my self-worth and tell myself the truth about my positive qualities. I had to change my mind, literally. I reprogrammed it by using positive self-talk and visualizations.

If you're going to be happy as you age (and you're going to age no matter what), be honest with yourself about who you really are and why you're doing what you're doing.

An acquaintance of mine is a fitness instructor. She recently had some plastic surgery done. Before deciding, she talked it over with family, friends, and clients. She very honestly said, "I need to do this for my self-esteem. My eyelids were making me look and feel tired all the time. I want to look and feel as vital as I believe I am. I will never lie when given a compliment about looking great. I don't mind saying that I've had some nips and tucks!" She was honest about her need for plastic surgery to help with her self-esteem. She didn't lie about it or try and cover it up.

It's not *what* you do to feel good about yourself, it's the *why* that's important. Make sure you're deeply aware of why you're doing something and that you tell yourself the truth.

Telling the truth also means remembering youth for what is was . . . not what modern advertising makes it out to be. It wasn't always sexy, glamorous, fun loving, carefree. Usually, we aren't as well off financially as the ads would have us believe. Do you truthfully remember your 20's? I do. Newly married, with a new career, trying to be the perfect wife, teacher, etc. Did I have confidence in my abilities? No. Did I think I was attractive and intelligent? No. Did I believe I was doing an excellent job? I knew I was trying extremely hard, but I also found myself constantly focusing on what I wasn't doing well, not on the positive. Does this sound familiar?

Most of us in our twenties are trying hard to be who and what we *think* we should be, but we don't have the inner confidence that comes with years of experience. We are trying to impress others or ourselves. We worry about what the Jones's, Smith's, our boss, our friends, and acquaintances will think and say. We dress like the fashion industry says we should. We don't wear shorts to the symphony, or formal attire to a barbecue, etc., because we've been taught that one shouldn't do those ill-mannered types of things. Is that happiness? Living according to someone else's rules or rituals keep us restricted. Is that a basis for accepting oneself? The answer is "No." When we constantly try and live all the should's and shouldn'ts that are given to us, it's no wonder we have a hard time accepting aging. We probably grew up not accepting who and what we were all along.

Today we live in a youth-obsessed society. Look at advertisements (except in publications targeted to seniors). Is there

"You never find yourself until you face the truth."
—Pearl Bailey

anyone over 35? We are bombarded with the beauty, sexiness, and success of youth. If we compare ourselves to this ideal, we are doomed to unhappiness as we age. We can pretend to have self-esteem. If we buy into the notion that youth is king, we will never be content with who and what we are now. We'll have to lie to ourselves in the process.

Tell the truth to yourself. You are not as young as you used to be. There are wrinkles and gray hairs. But have you thought recently about the most important part of your body—your mind? Aren't you wiser now? More confident of yourself and your abilities? As we age, we usually develop the confidence that we've lacked in our earlier years. Isn't that worth a lot? Our culture doesn't value it, but other cultures do and ancient cultures certainly valued the wisdom of the elders. It's time we went back to valuing our elders. The only way this will happen is when we, as elders, start valuing ourselves the way we are now.

Today, at 52, I feel better about myself and my life than I have at any other time in my life. Even when things are not going as I had hoped or when I'm feeling down about something, I am still happier now than ever before. After years of not believing in myself and hoping that "someday when . . ." I would arrive at

"The much sought after prize of eternal youth is just arrested development."
—Edgar Lee Masters

an end result, happiness, I finally realized that joy is not a desti-
nation. It's the journey that counts. At that point, I could tell
the truth about my sags, wrinkles, and other imperfections
and know that my life was what I made of it.

Once we give up the notion that youth is king, we can tell
ourselves the truth of who we are and what we are. We can miss
certain parts of our past (more energy, better memory, a
youthful body), but we can also focus on what we have gained
(confidence, experience, wisdom). When you start valuing your
true gifts, you will know the feeling of being ageless. No one
else can make this happen except you. Take responsibility for
changing your perspective and telling yourself the truth about
what a wise and wonderful person you are.

Telling the Truth Exercise:

Answer these questions honestly:

- Do I try to act younger than I really am? Why?
- Who am I trying to impress? Deceive? Fit in with?
- Do I focus on what I don't have? Can't do? Am not good at?
- Do I believe that life was better during my youth? Why?
- Do I really value my own wisdom? (If you don't, no one else
  will either.)

Strategies to Jump-start Solutions:

- If you find yourself trying to act younger, ask yourself, "What am I trying to recapture by doing this?" "Who am I trying to kid?" "Why can't I do what I want, act as I want to act, and still be happy with my age?"
- If you find you are trying to impress, deceive, or fit in with certain people, talk with them honestly, if you can. Tell them how you would really like to be. If they are honest, caring people, they will like you for who you are, not who you are trying to be. You can also slowly start to make the changes you want to make and watch their responses. Maybe it isn't a problem after all.
- If you are constantly focusing on the negative, see the chapter on attitude (Chapter 13).

Final Thoughts

If you cannot change your belief that life was best during your youth, you will struggle with the aging process. Using positive self-talk and/or working with a counselor, mentor, or clergy member will help you learn to value your own wisdom. Anyone who believes that right now is the best time of her or his life and who tells herself or himself the truth about her or his own wisdom has the ingredients necessary for being ageless.

THREE

Live in Sync with Your Values

❧

One of the best ways to help yourself give up the notion that youth is king is to live your values, those things that are most important to you. This means becoming *aware* of what these values are and *re-examining* your behavior. For example, you might say your health is important, yet you continue smoking. Either your deepest values do not include health, or your way of behaving is not in line with your values and, therefore, you are not living in sync with them. Sometimes you can live part of your life congruently with your values and struggle in other areas. The goal, however, is to behave in ways that match your deepest values in all realms of your life.

When you are living in line with your values, it is much easier to realize that youth is *not* king, that this idea is an illusion created by businesses and promoted in the media to accelerate sales and consumerism. When your values are clear and when you *act* accordingly, however, aging successfully is a natural by-product. You *know* what you are doing is best for you and, therefore, you are less likely to buy into the selling of youth. When you have a strong sense of your values and act congruently, life has meaning. There is pleasure at reaching goals, at living life with purpose. You become, in a sense, ageless.

When your actions are in line with your values, life also has more clarity. There is direction. It's easier to make choices in your best interest. You have a clear mind, a conscience that guides you. As Walt Disney's Jiminy Crickett said, "Let your conscience be your guide." Your conscience is what determines your real values. When your conscience and your actions are congruent, you know that what you are doing is right for you.

We originally get our values from our parents, other significant adults, our friends, our religion, and our culture. Usually we accept these without questioning whether or not they are right for us personally. Sometimes we may choose opposite values as a way of rebellion. Very few people take time during their lives to stop and think about what is truly important to them without something traumatic first being the catalyst.

This traumatic event is usually a loss—of a job, parent, spouse or partner, child, or our own or a loved one's health. This loss often leads us to actively examine our deepest-held values. When we begin to see how precious our day-to-day life is, we start reorganizing our values to put the emphasis on being happy with who, what, and where we are now.

When I was in my twenties, I didn't have goals. I only knew I wanted to be *the best*—wife, teacher, friend, and daughter. However, I didn't know how to go about achieving those bests, because they weren't real goals or even a set of values. Other than valuing hard work and giving everything of myself (often at the expense of myself), I just did my life without thinking. It was only after a divorce and leaving my safe and secure profession of teaching that I started reevaluating my life, understanding what values and goals were, and began to plan and create a life I loved.

We shouldn't feel guilty for choosing different values than our parents, religion, or society. We must be happy with who we are, with what we do, and how we spend our time and money. If our family or friends cannot accept us because we are now living in accordance with our deepest-held values (instead of theirs), then we must let them be as they are and continue to do what is right for ourselves. We can still continue our relationships and keep in contact with those who may differ in values, but we do not have to go against what we believe is in our best interest. Living congruently with our values helps us achieve the sense of agelessness because there is a deep peace of mind that comes from knowing that we are doing what is in our best interest.

Values Change

Our values will often change as we age. When we're in our twenties and thirties, we may put financial stability ahead of being with our family. We can be more easily swayed by the advertising campaigns that tell us we'll be happier, sexier, more alive if we buy product x, y, or z. The values of youth are not always the healthiest emotionally. For example, one value of youth is often instant gratification—"Buy it now." Is it always best to purchase something now, even if it means paying a large interest charge on your credit card? Or is waiting until you can afford something better for building character?

Another value of youth seems to be acquisition. If you continue to value acquiring *things* more than accepting and living your life with what you have now, you may find yourself struggling with and accepting aging. While it's wonderful to strive for

"A person doesn't become old until his regrets take the place of his dreams."
—John R. Noe

more and better, if you aren't happy with what you have now, you'll most likely find it difficult to be happy with what you acquire. Usually people who value acquiring things are unable to be happy with what they already have. They are constantly wanting more. How does this tie in? The similarity is this: If you are always wishing you were different (e.g., younger), you will find it hard to enjoy what life brings you now, at this age. The crucial point is that you will find greater happiness if you value who and what you are *now*.

When you accept yourself, you can value yourself. You find contentment that comes with peace of mind. When you feel the satisfaction of living in sync with your deepest values, you know you are living on purpose. These are qualities of being ageless.

Living in Sync with Your Values Exercise:

♦ Quickly write down the five things you value most. Don't spend a lot of time on this. Write what first comes to your mind. Then write five more.

♦ Are you living your life according to your highest values? How can you tell? (Look below at the "jump-start" section for a hint.)

♦ What values are you living that are *not* yours? Whose are they? Where did they come from? What can you do to begin to change your life to be better aligned with your own values?

Strategies to Jump-start Solutions:

- If you can't come up with at least five things that are the most important in your life, try this: Write the sentence, "_____ is *good*." Then fill in, as fast as you can, up to 100 things you believe are good. Take this list and narrow it down by writing, "_____ is *important*." Now come up with 25 items. From this, choose your top five or ten significant values.

- To check yourself to find out if you are living your life according to your values, look back at your answers to the first question. Then open your checkbook, get out your credit card statements and your datebook. If you are spending the majority of your time and money on those items that you *state* are your highest values, then you are living your life accordingly. If not, one or the other (stated values or time and money spent) must be changed for you to begin living your life in sync.

- If you notice that you are living someone else's values, you might feel worried about making a dramatic change immediately. If this is the case, break down the changes you want to make into small chunks or steps. For example, if you realize that the church you attend does not practice loving behavior, which is in sync with your deepest values, you might start by writing down all the alternative possibilities. Then list the steps in finding a way to meet your spiritual

"Old age is like everything else. To make a success of it, you've got to start young."
—Fred Astaire

needs. By doing this, you can then find a suitable way of finding what you want, rather than just quitting the church and feeling the serious loss without first discovering and/or exploring all the alternatives.

Final Thoughts

You can more easily give up believing that youth is king when you value yourself and live your life in sync with your deepest-held values. You know you are letting your conscience be your guide and you are being *true to yourself*. This, in turn, creates a sense of inner peace. This inner peace is a part of aging successfully.

"Just remember when you're over the hill, you begin to pick up speed."
—Charles Schultz

FOUR

Take Responsibility for Your Life

❧

If you are going to live agelessly, it's important to take responsibility for your own life. This means that when circumstances don't turn out the way you want them to, you must look at *your* responsibility in addition to the other people, things, and circumstances involved. If you tend to blame others and play the victim, your challenge is to look at your own part —honestly and fairly. If you tend to be super-responsible and always blame yourself, your task is to see what other variables were present to create the current situation—keenly and without piling the guilt on yourself.

I started out life as one who always blamed herself. I could have been an innocent bystander, but I still would have somehow believed I was at fault. Talk about living with guilt, sadness, and grief! It was completely dis-empowering. No wonder I didn't have good self-esteem. Who would, if they were the cause of *all* the problems in the world?

Gradually, I learned that every negative situation wasn't my fault. I realized every situation has at least two sides, if not several contributing factors. This realization helped me stop the inward torment and choose to *respond* in a way that acknowledged both (or all) parties. I learned how to be "response-able" in a different way.

There are two parts to being responsible. The first is the typical definition—asking yourself, "What was my part here? What choices and decisions did I make that led me to being here now?" In other words, not blaming someone or something else for the outcome. There are influences and variables that none of us can control, of course, but to blame an outcome on another person or thing is not taking control of your life.

When you feel out of control, you are a lot less happy with life because you feel always at the mercy of others. When you start behaving as if you have choices (and you do), then you will feel much more in control of circumstances. When something goes wrong, you can see what part you played in the outcome. If you want to live life in an ageless manner, you can then ask yourself, "So what can I learn here?" or "What gift might I receive from this turn of events?"

When you do that, and learn from whatever the results are, you will continue to grow and change your life for the better. This is an important aspect of being ageless—learning from whatever you can to better your life (and, as a by-product, the lives of others around you). This is simple, but not easy to do. Until it becomes a habit, it takes a concerted effort to retrain your mind to think in that way, but it is worth the effort. Peace of mind and gratitude are the results.

The second part of being responsible that will help you to age successfully is "response-ability." This is when you *choose* your response to any situation. In other words, you have the ability to respond to circumstances any way you want. By responding in a way that supports you and honors the others involved, you are taking "response-ability."

Responding and reacting are two different things. How we react is an automatic, unconscious behavior. We may initially feel angry or sad when we hear something. That's our reaction. But it's what we do with that reaction that then becomes our response.

"Nothing ages people like not thinking."
—Christopher Morley

Our responses are, therefore, the *conscious decisions* we make. In other words, we can't control the initial reaction (emotion), but we can control the subsequent response (action).

When events turn out differently than planned, can you respond gracefully? You may react strongly, but can you then assert yourself by explaining your feelings and thoughts calmly and with thoughtful behavior? It is important to honor all your feelings, not to deny them. But it is equally important to do so in a way that honors others as well.

Taking Responsibility for Your Life Exercise:

* What is your typical response when something goes wrong? Do you usually play the victim by blaming other people, things, or events? Do you always see yourself as being the culprit, even when others are involved, and become a victim of yourself? Whatever your typical response, realize that responsibility is shared.
* Look back on some recent event that did not turn out as planned. Were you able to learn something from the outcome? Can you retrace your decisions and choices that led you to that moment? If not, do that now. Every situation presents something to be learned. To learn and grow is a sign of being ageless.

Strategies to Jump-start Solutions:

- If your typical response is blaming, the next time this happens ask yourself, "What is *my* responsibility here? What decisions did I make to lead me to this place in time?"
- If your typical response is to shoulder all the responsibility, ask yourself: "Who (or what) else is involved here? What parts did they (it) play?"
- If you have a hard time finding something to learn or ways to grow from mistakes or things going wrong, write this question on two 3×5 cards: "What can I learn here?" Place one on your desk at work and one on your refrigerator door. Ponder the question whenever needed.

Final Thoughts

To be ageless, respond to circumstances that are less than you had hoped for by acknowledging your feelings and the shared responsibility of all parties. Exercise your "response-ability" and choose a response that honors yourself and others.

"The Golden Age is not behind, but before us."
—Saint-Simon Louis de Rouvroy

FIVE

Assert Yourself

In order to give up the idea that youth is king, you must assert yourself. This means you've got to be able to go against the tide of the media, society, and even, perhaps, friends and family in order to maintain your stance that aging is a beautiful and positive experience. It may take years and a majority of elders to turn around the tide of negativity about aging portrayed in the media, but it *will* happen, and you can be at the forefront of this movement by asserting yourself in several ways.

First, assert yourself by believing that aging is "becoming." This is meant as a double entendre. Aging is (a) becoming truer to yourself, becoming more of who you are, plus, (b) "becoming" as in beautiful. When you start being yourself, there is joy in the sense of freedom that comes with living life as you want. When you start believing that beauty is more than skin deep, your confidence automatically grows because you know your self-worth is more than the outside packaging.

Secondly, you can assert yourself by standing up for what you believe is right, honest, and necessary for your own good. For example, if a doctor says you need a certain operation, and you believe that another less intrusive form of medical treatment is best, then you must assert yourself. How? In this case, seek out a second or even third opinion. By asserting your needs, you take control of your life. You realize you are the one responsible, which leads to peace of mind.

Thirdly, you must assert yourself in making the necessary changes in your own life that will support your healthy aging, such as eating nutritious meals, exercising, and/or taking vitamin and mineral supplements. Do not expect to treat your body with disrespect and have it age well. That is not a realistic expectation.

Dealing with Others

There are times when it is appropriate to be passive and times when it is appropriate to be aggressive, but too often people respond to situations with one of these two extremes when the middle road of assertiveness is the best option. Sometimes we need to let the other person have his or her way, but we need to assert what we believe is best first. Sometimes we need to take control when we are certain about what must be done, but we need to listen to what others have to say first. Being assertive is stating or asking for what you want in a way that does not bully another person nor give yourself away.

If you are not normally assertive and usually let others have their way, there are many possible reasons why. Perhaps you fear hurting someone's feelings or being rejected. You may have been taught that passive behavior is the proper and best way to be, or you may not want to deal with someone's anger. By not being assertive, however, you are giving up a part of yourself. Each time you do not speak up for what you need or want, a little piece of you dies inside, metaphorically.

When you are passive, your lack of assertion can come to haunt you, often in resentment. You may cut yourself off from the people to whom you gave yourself away. When you are passive, one of three things will usually happen:

1. You will either find unconscious ways to do what you wanted anyway or,

"I've done more harm by the falseness of trying to please than by the honesty of trying to hurt."

—Jessamyn West

2. If you push resentment down inside of you, it can fester and grow where it could come out like a volcano, at an inappropriate time or,

3. The resentment or unhappiness can stay submerged, eat away at you, and later show up as illness.

This is the pattern I grew up with—being passive; putting everyone else's needs first and giving away myself in order to please. I was afraid of hurting others' feelings, of their anger, and I was also afraid I wasn't smart enough to trust what I thought was best. I kept my own thoughts cramped down and eventually they would show up in an illness, usually asthma. At that time, it was the only way I could express my true feelings of frustration, fear, or anger.

If you are normally passive, you will need to learn to have the courage to speak up. This often comes as a direct result of believing in yourself.

If you have been aggressive in your past, being assertive will also be a challenge, but in a different way. You may have become this way because you were bullied yourself in the past and need to feel in control, or you could have patterned yourself after a parent or significant older person in your life. You could also have become aggressive as a rebellion to being around passive elders and seeing them giving up their needs and desires. You will need to take into account the needs of others and learn to moderate your responses. You will need to find ways to negotiate compromises instead of simply bullying your way around to get what you want. When you are aggressive, you often end up pushing away people you care about, work with, or who may be important to you later.

You may initially feel great because you get your way. You may think you're always right. But, eventually, you'll notice that you aren't looked up to because of your wisdom but followed be-cause of fear. Life is pretty lonely when you have to have things your way—when you can't collaborate with others and when you can't listen to what others are saying without maintaining your superiority.

Whether you have passive or aggressive tendencies, asserting yourself in a straightforward, calm, and confident manner is the key.

Asserting Yourself Exercise:
- Think about when you and someone else each wanted some-thing different. How did you handle it? Did you state

"The way to stay young is to keep in the game."
—Dr. Frank Crane

what you wanted in clear terms? Or did you say to yourself something like, "Oh well, I'm not going to get what I want anyway. It's nicer to just keep quiet and let him or her have what he or she wants."? Or did you insist that your way was right and needed to be done, "period, end of discussion"? Think about other examples, too. We all can change our ways if we are committed to doing so. Think through enough past situations so you know your normal patterns.

- How do you handle it when your family and friends, religious community, or culture have implicit rules or procedures that are not compatible to your way? Are you assertive in going against them, do you comply when around others but do as you wish when on your own, or do you think and do what you believe is best without imposing your way on others? Think about whether or not you are assertive in the bigger picture.

- Do you have the willpower and assertiveness to change your old habits (which will, in turn, help you age successfully)? In other words, can you assert yourself on an intrapersonal basis (with yourself) to make positive lifestyle changes?

Strategies to Jump-start Solutions:
- If you are not naturally or have not learned to be assertive, you can learn now. There are books that describe how to

become assertive; however, as a start, here are some ideas for both passive and aggressive people:

- If you are normally passive, then before saying, "Yes," "Okay," or "That's all right," stop and take a breath, literally! The next step is to say, "Let me think about this." This pause will give you the time to say, "No" or whatever else you might need to say. Learn to believe that you are as worthy as anyone else, and you deserve to have what you want, too.

- If you are normally aggressive, you also need to stop and take a breath. Then count to ten and, as you do, realize that your view is not the only one that is real. At this time, try putting yourself in the other person's shoes. With all your concentration, imagine seeing the situation from his or her standpoint. Think of how you (or anyone) could benefit from a different outcome than the one you want. Then calmly state your desires and truly listen to his or hers. Try and come to a compromise, if possible.

Final Thoughts

In order to give up on the notion that youth is king, you will need to be assertive against the tide of this culture—that life is best when young. To be assertive here also means to believe in your self-worth. Believe that the best time in life is right *now*, or if it isn't the very best time at this specific moment, then, at least notice the good and positive aspects of life—no matter what your age and condition.

As an aging adult, you will feel far happier when you can assert your needs, simply, calmly, and peacefully. When you are able to assert yourself, you will notice a deep sense of confidence and satisfaction with your life. The way to begin that process is to be keenly aware of who and what you are.

Acknowledge Reality

SIX

Become Aware of You

❧

Accepting the aging process is important not only on the intellectual level, but also on the emotional one. It is easy to acknowledge aging intellectually, but until you really know who you are, it will be much more difficult to accept it emotionally. When you emotionally acknowledge your own aging, you will be able to embrace that ageless quality.

While this has some relationship to the second chapter on telling yourself the truth, this point goes a step deeper. When you tell yourself the truth about your good and bad points, you also need to look at such things as what *really* motivates you to do what you do. What "old tapes" or old ideas have held you back even though they no longer work for you? What dreams and desires have you given up because you've become disenchanted with your life?

Many people are motivated out of fear, even though they won't admit it. When one chooses ease or comfort over taking a risk, there is usually a fear beneath it. What fears motivate you? Are you afraid of hurting someone's feelings? Afraid of being turned down, rejected, abandoned? Afraid you will fail, or, perhaps, succeed? Afraid you can't live up to others' opinions of you (or your opinion of yourself)?

Most of us have some of these motivating fears. I've never met anyone who is immune. Some people easily take physical risks. They try something new, like skiing or rock climbing, without a second thought. But they stumble when it comes to emotional risk taking. They are afraid to leave an unhealthy relationship or to begin a new one. They are afraid to look for a job in a new area or quit the job they have for fear they won't find one as good. Some people are the opposite; they can take emotional risks more easily than they can physical ones.

When you know who you are at the deepest level, you will then be able to make the changes necessary to better your life, in this case, becoming ageless. Being honest about yourself is the key here. Without gut-wrenching honesty, you will only be deceiving yourself. Get to know yourself in all realms—physically, mentally, emotionally, and spiritually. Find out your strongest motivations. This is the beginning of the journey of aging successfully.

When you know your greatest motivating factors, you will then be able to move beyond your fears; you'll be able to take more risks (even if they're small ones) and you'll be compelled to live your dreams. This is actually one of the most exciting aspects about the second half of your life. Usually people reassess their lives and realize that there are some dreams that never came to fruition. Some will shrug their shoulders and give up, living lives of "quiet desperation." Others will, instead, take the challenge and basically say to themselves, "Well, if I don't do this *now*, when will I ever do it?" They either jump in feet first or they at least wade in ankle-deep and test the water, aiming at their long-cherished goals.

These people are living their lives joyfully. They realize that after they've become aware of who they are, they must make positive changes in order to avoid the resentment and bitterness that stem from a life not lived to its fullest potential. Those who decide to know themselves in complete honesty— their pluses and minuses—and who choose to do something with this knowledge, will find the contentment that is available to each of us, if we take this step.

"Until you make peace with who you are, you'll never be content with what you have."
—Doris Mortman

I was in my mid-to-late thirties when I started to become aware of the real me. I found myself discontent in a solid marriage. I was unhappy with a secure job. It didn't make sense to me, but I knew some things needed changing. Even though the picture looked perfect on the outside, my insides knew that the real me was being stifled. What I learned over years of working with counselors, coaches, and mentors, reading every self-help book I could find, and attending workshops and seminars was that when I took bold steps to move toward the life I wanted—when I would be motivated internally—doors would open. I would, in every instance, find the support to make the next step on my personal journey.

Becoming Aware of You Exercise:

- List what you consider to be your positive and negative traits. What have you done to enlarge the positive and eliminate or modify the negative ones?
- What are the things that motivate you? If you say money, go deeper and ask yourself what money means to you (e.g., comfort, freedom, power). Do the same whatever you answer, whether it is security, peace of mind, fear. Keep asking yourself (and writing the answers to), "What does this mean to me?" Eventually, you'll find your strongest internal motivators. Knowing these motivating factors is important to living a joyful life at any age.

- What does being ageless mean to you? What can you do to enhance your own aging process?

Strategies to Jump-start Solutions:
- If you can't see yourself clearly, ask others. This time, ask not only family and friends, but also ask employers, colleagues, tennis partners, or others who are not as close to you as family members are. If you haven't done anything for your own growth and positive change, start reading or join organizations or groups that will support your growth. Work with coaches, mentors, or therapists to move beyond where you are now. These resources can help either by teaching you necessary life skills or by giving you the kind of honest feedback you may need to hear.
- If you find you are not pleased about what motivates you (e.g., mostly fear), then make a point of trying something just for the sheer joy of it, simply because you love doing it. Or first try taking a very small risk. Notice how good it feels to succeed, or if it failed, that your world didn't end because of it. Continue to take small risks and work your way up to bigger risks.
- When you find your positive motivators, keep a list of them handy. Draw upon them when you want to take a leap in a new direction and use them. (For example, if rewarding

"We are the hero of our own story."
—Mary McCarthy

yourself with a new piece of clothing or a massage works, use that to take a risk.) Even if it's a negative motivator—like the fear of being unemployed—use that to push yourself beyond your complacency.

- If you can't define what ageless aging means to you, you'll have a hard time doing it. Talk with close friends and loved ones. Let these discussions help you discover your meaning. Then you can take this information and use it as a guide to change your behavior, to start new projects, and/or to reach out to those that you want to connect with. It will be your benchmark to support you in feeling ageless.

Final Thoughts

No one can define exactly what being ageless means to anyone else, yet there are some common characteristics that are the foundation for this book. You have to believe in your own definition of the term in order to move toward it. Once you have your own definition, you can use that as a road map to help direct your energies to becoming what you aspire to be. Learning your internal motivators will help you reach your goals. Becoming aware of who you are *now* is your starting point for a journey of aging joyfully.

"We're always the same age inside."
—Gertrude Stein

SEVEN

Accept the Inevitability of Aging

❧

In all the interviews of people I believed were aging happily, the one word that came up most often was "accept." Acceptance is one of the most important keys to becoming ageless. To put it simply, accept that you are getting older. What is important as well is not to confuse getting older with getting worse. That is buying into the myth of youth as king. Realize that growing older *is* a part of life, as is dying.

We've somehow carried the "Great American Fairytale" too far. This fairytale, begun in the 1950's and, with repercussions still evident today, goes like this: Boy meets girl, they fall in love, and they get married. Man has a career in a company where he'll work loyally for 30 years. They buy a house in the suburbs. Wife stays home and takes care of the two children (one boy and one girl, of course). He retires and receives a gold watch. Life is happy-ever-after. No problems, no worries, no strife. The implied continuation of this fairytale seems to say we don't age and never die. As ridiculous as this seems, I believe, the underlying ideas are still in our collective psyche. We not only don't have lifetime jobs or marriages any more (at least the majority of us don't), but we also are going to age and die no matter what kind of a life we have led.

When you accept that aging is a natural process, it's easier to stop worrying about the wrinkles. You know they are natural. You stop worrying about slowing down. It will happen and it will be okay. It's when you live in *denial* of your aging that you suffer. If you refuse to accept the aging process, you may feel an emotional charge with each new physical change. This is because your wrinkles may bother you; your joints, which don't move as easily as before, may bother you; your weaker digestive system may bother you. Every part of your life may contribute to your worries and fears. While it is important *not* to deny the real pain of arthritis or other ailments (and to do what you can to make positive changes), it is equally important to *accept* the inevitability of the way your body changes as you age.

When you accept the aging process, you then decide, as one 70-year-old told me, to "love your wrinkles," rather than lament the fact that so-and-so has better genes and her skin is more youthful. You decide not to stay out as late, drink as much as you used to, or go out in the sun.

As I was taking a shuttle from Boise, Idaho, to Sun Valley, the three-hour drive along the stark, high desert highway gave me time to get to know the other passengers. Since this was a mid-week morning, there were only two—a couple in their seventies. I was going on a writing retreat; they were going skiing. They made this trip, from Bermuda where they lived, several times each winter. Obviously, they were avid skiers. When I talked about my book, they said, "We've got no complaints. Our life is good. Sure, we don't ski as hard and long as we used to. We 'ballroom ski' instead. You know, sort of waltzing down the slopes instead of pushing ourselves. Sometimes we take mid-day naps. We haven't given up what we love doing; we've just changed *how* we do it!"

They accepted what is and made their life work around it. It's that simple (though it may not always be easy). When you can emotionally accept the inevitability of aging, your attitude will

> "When grace is joined with wrinkles, it is admirable."
> —Victor Hugo

lighten—that is another one of the biggest keys to being age-less (see Chapter 13). By accepting what is, you are not giving up, nor are you resisting. Giving up means resigning yourself to an existence and having no joy, love, or hope about the present or future. Resistance, on the other hand, is pushing against (or beating your head against) the brick wall of life, instead of going around, over, under it, or stepping back and looking for a door, which you may have missed. Resisting aging, such as worrying about how old you look, will simply add more wrinkles!

Once you accept the inevitability of aging, you can then set about discerning for yourself what is right for you.

Accepting the Inevitability of Aging Exercise:

◆ Are you accepting your own aging? Are you accepting the aging of those around you—your parents, kids, friends, and colleagues? What thoughts come to mind when you think of getting older? Whatever your first answers were, that will give you a hint of your truth.

◆ When you notice your wrinkles and/or your stiffness in the morning (or some other sign of aging), what do you do? Or want to do? How do you feel and what are your thoughts?

Strategies to Jump-start Solutions:

- If you are finding it difficult to accept your own aging, finish this book first. Then volunteer at a senior center. Sign up for an Elderhostel program and observe the seniors who take them. Make a point to learn something, not just from the course itself, but from the other participants. Your peers can be your best teachers.

- Ask yourself, "How can I take care of myself to prevent unnecessary wrinkles or aches and pains?" For example, stay out of the sun and use strong sunscreen when you are in it. Use a moisturizer that keeps your skin supple. Make stretching a regular part of your daily habit. It will help ease aches and pains. If your joints are aching, ask a health-care practitioner about stretching techniques or nutritional supplements that may help. Taking care of yourself through prevention is common sense and can help relieve some of the worries of aging.

Final Thoughts

For many people, talking about their feelings (Chapter 10) helps them to accept the aging process and to change any negative thoughts that they may have. Noticing the positive (Chapter 13) and living in the moment (Chapter 15) can also help you accept the inevitability of the aging process. These are some of the most important keys for feeling the peace of mind that comes with being ageless.

EIGHT

Discern the Wisest Choices

❧

Sometimes, especially as we age, decision-making can be more difficult than usual. It is important to use discernment when you make choices. Discernment means being able to differentiate between several options that all seem like possible solutions. What will help you the most is:

1. Making sure you uncover as many options as you can (not just believing in only black or white answers);
2. Knowing your resources, personal values, and passions;
3. Realizing the best time to act on your decisions; and
4. Making whatever you choose a winning scenario.

When you believe there are only two solutions to the problem, go beyond those self-imposed limits and brainstorm (with yourself and/or others) for creative ideas. There are almost always *more* possible solutions to any issue than we originally thought.

There are ways to expand your options by expanding your mind—bringing in the natural creativity that we all have. This is creative problem-solving. (See the strategies that follow.) The more options you have available, the better your chances of finding a solution that works best.

It's also important to know what resources are available to you, both internal and external—in other words, your own personal assets and those of other people and organizations. These will help you see the bigger picture. You've had a lot of experience in your life; that's one of the gifts of age. Use your knowledge and experiences to move past your first obvious choices. Then tap into the resources of friends, family, and co-workers. This can even be fun. Have a brainstorming party or a conference call. The more heads you've got working on a creative solution, the better.

Being aware of your values and passions—the people and things, the beliefs and concepts that are most important to you—will also help. This way you will always have a benchmark from which to measure your choices. With every important decision you make, remember your priorities. Whatever decision you make, ask yourself, "Is this supporting (or hindering) my progress toward my most important goals, dreams, and desires?" If your decision supports your forward movement, then you know it's right. If it is taking you in another direction, ask yourself, "Am I ready to change my values and goals to be in line with this decision, or do I need to rethink my decision?"

Timing is always crucial for making the best choices. For example, you may want to move to another city. This may fit with your values and desires and seem to be the perfect solution to the problems that you are facing now. However, if you do not allow the timing to occur naturally, it could end up seeming like the wrong decision. Trying to force a decision (moving, in this case) to happen too soon could cause more emotional pain than your original problem.

If you are in the middle of deep grief, anger, shame, or fear (or *any* other intense emotion), it is unwise to make and follow through on a major life decision. If you want to change a significant portion of your life, make sure your emotions are clear and calm. Make sure, too, that you have given yourself some time and space between a traumatic event and making the final decision. This is not to say that doing something different wouldn't be right. It might be. However, it is important to know that rash decisions, especially when made under emotional duress, can easily be regretted. In emotional times, we often

"Full maturity ...is achieved by realizing that you have choices to make."
—Angela Barron McBride

make choices to avoid more immediate pain rather than what might be best. Choices made to avoid emotional pain often cause more sorrow later. It's much healthier to experience the painful feelings and process your emotions fully. Once you are out of the depths of your pain, revisit the choice you made and then decide if it is still what you want to do.

During times when you are feeling intense emotions about one concern in your life, keep your ideas about what to do in your mind as possibilities and let them simmer. Wait. Later, ask trusted friends or loved ones for feedback. However, don't let their fears or narrow thinking keep you from making a bold change either. Let their views give you some balance and a different perspective rather than being the deciding factor.

Gerry, one of my clients, had recently been downsized out of her job. She was in her mid-fifties and felt that she couldn't get a new job because she was too old, even though she was highly trained. She had been divorced for many years and her children were in college or married. She had a beloved brother she was very close to who lived in another state and she was ready to move. Through questioning, she came to realize that it would be best to weather this emotional storm, do temporary work while she looked for full-time employment, and see what would happen in 6 months to a year. One year later, she had several offers to work for big corporations and recognized that she had loved the freedom of working for herself. Instead of working for someone else, she began a consulting business that today is thriving. She still misses not having her brother living close by, but she's thrilled with her new life. Now she even has more time for vacations to visit him.

Lastly, making your choice a winning situation is all about making your decision one that you can live with happily. This is such an important aspect of making choices that it has its own chapter, Chapter 14.

Discerning the Wisest Choices Exercise:

Think of several *major* decisions you made in the past five years. Look at the bulleted questions below and discover whether or not you considered all of the important aspects when making those choices.

* What was the decision?
* What available resources supported you (internal and external, people, money, space, organizations)?
* What were the most important considerations (your values and passions) that you needed to take into account before making this decision?

"Nature gives you the face you have at twenty; it's up to you to merit the face you have at fifty."
—Coco Chanel

- What options did you find immediately?
- Did you come up with three or more choices? If yes, which ideas did you develop through brainstorming?
- What new possibilities emerged after brainstorming techniques were used?
- What did your gut or intuition say about the available choices?

Next, think of a decision that needs to be made now or in the near future and do this again with the same questions.

Strategies to Jump-start Solutions:
- If you are stuck and believe that there aren't any external resources available to you, make a list of friends, family members, and colleagues, then call each person and ask who or what might be a resource for you in making this specific decision.
- If you feel you don't have the internal resources, either use the list above and select one or more of your dearest friends and/or family members to call for support and encouragement, or seek the help of a professional therapist, coach, or clergy.
- If you are not sure about what your deepest values and passions are, go back to the chapter entitled, "Live in Sync with Your Values" (Chapter 3), and do the values clarification

"The mere sense of living is joy enough."
—Emily Dickenson

exercises and come back to your decisions after reviewing your values.

Brainstorming techniques to use alone, when you can't tap the resources of others, are listed below. They are several of the best for stretching your mind and opening yourself up to new possibilities. These are not only excellent tools for becoming more creative in finding solutions, they are also fun and can be used for *any* kind of problem-solving.

- Ask yourself a silly question, such as one that a very young child might ask. For example, if you are trying to decide whether or not you want to buy a particular condominium, a child may want to know, "Why do you want to buy a condo anyway?" or "What's wrong with the house you have?" or "Why not buy a house on wheels if you like to travel so much?"

- Think of a person you admire for his or her wisdom. This person can be dead or alive, known to you personally, or someone who is famous. Find a quiet place where you can have a few moments undisturbed. Relax, close your eyes, take some deep breaths, and then ask this person what answers he or she would find to your problem. These answers may or may not lead you to a better conclusion. (They most often do, *if* you allow yourself to be open to the possibilities that will come from these types of questions.) Either way, they will stretch your mind and that will help you in making your choices.

* Meditate on your question. Many inventors have said that it is in that state halfway between waking and sleeping that they have discovered their best ideas.
* Write down the exact opposite of what you believe you want. It is often in writing down what you *don't* want that you begin to more clearly define what you do want.
* Trust your gut. Listen to that feeling inside that says, "Ooh, this seems exciting" or "Something just doesn't feel right about this." Your intuition, when you are able to access it, will always make the best choice for you.

Final Thoughts

In order to make the wisest decisions, be open to creative problem-solving and give yourself at least three selections, instead of the typical "a" or "b" choices that people normally give themselves. Know what your values are, as well as what your best resources may be. Next, be aware of timing in discerning the best choices. Timing can be crucial in making any choice a good one. Lastly, your attitude in making the decision a winning one is important and is discussed in Chapter 14.

NINE

Honor Your Body and Body-Time

 ❧

When you are able to honor your body and your body-time, it will support you in becoming ageless. This means realizing that your body won't always be able to do things the way it did in the past, with the same timing, frequency, intensity, or clarity. Unfortunately, many people label this "not as good," or "less than" and judge themselves this way. What happens as soon as we start to judge ourselves in a negative way is that our confidence, belief in ourselves, and our self-worth all decline.

Instead, honor your body and body-time, understanding that it may take you longer to recover from a late night out, a strenuous hike, or an intense project. You simply allow yourself the time it takes to recover without judging it as bad. You could also decide not to do some of the things you did when you were younger (such as over-indulging) and realize that these are wise and healthy choices you are now making.

This seems like such a simple way to look at life, yet so many people are critical of themselves because of the changes in their body and its timing. Who says that it's bad to need glasses for reading? Who says it's not as good to need more rest after staying out late? (In other words, what's wrong with a lingering morning in bed?) And, isn't it okay if you take naps midday? There is nothing wrong in slowing down.

A recent study found that joint injuries among baby-boomers were 43% higher in recent years than in previous ones. The conclusion was that this group had not stretched, warmed up before, or cooled down after exercising. In other words, they still believed their bodies were the same as when they were in their twenties. Not only is it good to honor our bodies and be nonjudgmental about what we need, it's also important for our overall safety and health.

I have always been a slow mover. I would never win races as a kid, but I always fell gracefully. (That was how I would justify being called a slow poke.) Even now as I slow down more, I

> *"The thing you are ripening toward is the fruit of your life."*
> —Stewart Edward White

look at the benefits of being this way. I've had to learn how to change my perspective so that I wouldn't beat myself up for what could be considered a fault. Now when I become aware of my slowness, I tell myself that this way I can stop and notice the small things in life. That doesn't mean I don't get frustrated from time to time when I want to do more than I have the time for, but my disadvantage as a child has helped me be okay with the slower time frames that I live in as I get older.

We live in a rush-rush world now. Trying to do everything at this high speed of life isn't healthy, no matter what your age. Doing what needs to be done with care and time is much more relaxing and joyful. It will also help you focus on what *truly* is important, because you will be making choices about how you spend your valuable time.

"You are never too old to become younger."
—Mae West

Changing your mind-set about what is good about being slower, versus judging yourself as bad or worse off, will make life much more enjoyable. It is buying into the youth is king myth that gets us to judge ourselves this way. To honor your body-time is to luxuriate in the beauty of the slowness. This is part of growing older gracefully, of believing in the concept of being ageless.

Honoring Your Body and Body-Time Exercise:

- What thoughts or feelings do you have when you notice it takes longer to recover from something strenuous? What happens when you realize that you can't do something that you were able to do when you were younger? Do you judge yourself in negative ways, or wish you could be younger?
- Can you imagine slowing down and doing activities joyfully, without stressing about what isn't getting done?

Strategies to Jump-start Solutions:

- If you find yourself constantly judging yourself negatively when it takes you longer to accomplish something, or wishing you were younger, then stop and take a deep breath. Notice the details of what you are doing in the moment (Chapter 15) and be grateful for whatever you have right now (Chapter 19).
- If you believe that you must keep up the crazy pace that is going on around you, then take a few moments and visualize the world moving at *your* pace. Actually imagine the joy if everyone did things more slowly, paying attention to the details of their lives. Realize that life is richer when it is lived at a pace where we can be in each moment.

Final Thoughts

You *can* be ageless when you stop judging your body and its timing against what it was like when you were younger. When you give yourself the time that is needed to do whatever it is that you want to do, you'll feel the enjoyment of being alive in the moment. You will be able to appreciate who you are *now*.

TEN

Acknowledge and Respect the Emotions of Aging

⤫

The emotions of aging are the emotions of change. They are the feelings of loss. Whenever things change in a big way in our life, we must deal with letting go of the old, a limbo period in between and acquiring the new. This is true whether it's letting go of something material, relational, or conceptual.

Though emotions do not come and go in any particular order, one of the first is grief. We are grieving our youth. We are grieving the way we used to be and behave. It will be normal to feel sadness from time to time with your aging. Whenever you can accept this or any other of the emotions of aging, you will pass through the emotion more easily and more quickly.

Other emotions bound to show up include anger, depression, fear, loneliness, anxiety, joy, delight, love, serenity, shame, guilt, and acceptance. These are the main emotions of aging, but any emotion that occurs can be part of the normal letting go and renewal process.

Think about why these emotions happen. You may be angry or ashamed, for example, because you can no longer run as fast, drink as much, sleep as peacefully, walk as long. You may fear death or becoming so ill that you could become incapacitated and not able to function as independently as you once did.

Depression and anxiety can happen for the same reasons as fear. When we realize we aren't who we used to be, we can either become depressed or accept it. If you are able to go through all the emotions of aging, change, and loss, then you will ultimately come to acceptance, which is the healthiest place to be.

When I was 47, I went through a year-long period feeling alternately grief and sadness with some resentment and anger on the side. It all started one morning looking in the mirror after being on a jet for over fourteen hours and waking up extremely jet-lagged. Of course, I looked awful. I was beginning my business in Europe and it was scary to be on foreign ground, starting all over again. I was afraid, exhausted, and sleep-deprived. What I saw in the mirror horrified me. Who was this old hag? I saw wrinkles, sags, and pasty skin tone that I swear had never been there before. I saw the woman I thought I would be in, maybe, another ten or fifteen years, not *now*. I was feeling the typical emotions of aging. That began a time period of reassessing my life; reevaluating my physical self and coming to terms with my new self. A year later, I came to the conclusion that I looked darn good for my age. I now proudly state how old I am whenever asked (and sometimes even when I'm not).

Joy, peace, and acceptance are emotions that you can also feel as you age, because you are realizing that the best moments of your life are *now* and you *make* them that way. You find the good in your life and keep the positive attitude that is needed.

The most important point, however, about acknowledging and respecting the emotions of aging is to realize that feeling any and all of these emotions is normal and is part of the process of growing older. Once you know this, then you can be kind to yourself and say, "Oh, this (emotion) is just a part of being ageless." Whenever you judge yourself as bad or think that something is wrong because you feel any of these emotions, you then get stuck in that emotion, making the feeling last longer. If you let an emotion be okay from the start, you will be able to move through it more easily.

To feel ageless, understand and respect your emotions; know that they are all normal and let yourself experience them. For many people, it is also important to express them. When you express them, it is important to do so in a way that respects and honors the others involved. Not acknowledging or experiencing your emotions can be risky in two ways. Feelings repressed for too long can bubble up at the wrong time or with the wrong person. Or, emotions can fester inside for so long that they actually make you ill. Researchers now know the mind has a powerful effect on the body. Many doctors and other health-care practitioners believe that 70% to 90% of all illness has a stress-related component. When you are not able to experience your feelings, this becomes an emotional stress.

Acknowledging, respecting, and experiencing your emotions are important to achieving agelessness. Once you have worked through the emotions, you are able to be at peace with yourself. Then you can let go of the old images of yourself and what your life "should" be like. The results are happiness with who and where you are now.

> *"I make the most of all that comes and the least of all that goes."*
> —Sara Teasdale

Acknowledging the Emotions of Aging Exercise:

- What kinds of emotions have you felt as you've noticed yourself aging?
- What do you do when you begin feeling the negative emotions? What do you say to and about yourself then?
- Do you try and deny or repress negative emotions? If so, what happens with them? Do they come out at inappropriate times or with innocent people? Or do you keep them completely submerged?

Strategies to Jump-start Solutions:

- If you were stumped and couldn't think of any emotions that you've been feeling about your aging, perhaps it's time to dig deeper inside. We all have emotions, but for some, realizing what they are, is a struggle. Start by noticing what your thoughts are about aging. Then ask yourself what feelings these thoughts *might* provoke and decide which of the emotions fit for you. (To help decide if a word is an emotion or not, if you can fit the word "think" into the same sentence, it is not an emotion.)
- If you think of yourself as bad or immature for having negative feelings, as soon as you catch yourself putting yourself down, stop and tell yourself, "This is normal. It is good that I am aware and experiencing my emotions." Keep saying this as often as necessary until you begin believing it.

- If you know what you're feeling, but don't express them, at least allow yourself to experience them in some way. Try writing them down. If you need to do something, such as beating a pillow or jogging the emotions out of your system before you express them, then do that. Next, decide if you need to change your attitude or deal with the issue that caused the emotions. Changing your attitude means deciding that whatever the issue is, it isn't worth putting any more time or energy into it. If it is something that is of greater importance, deal with it—talk to the person(s) who are involved or take some action to solve the problem. The critical point here is to first acknowledge the emotion and then experience it in a way that works for you. Then you can choose how to deal with the issues that triggered your emotions.

Final Thoughts

When you can acknowledge and respect the emotions of aging, you will realize you are going through a normal process that happens with any kind of change or loss. Experience your feelings and know you can become ageless when you accept yourself and all of your emotions.

"After a certain number of years, our faces become our biography."
—Cynthia Ozick

ELEVEN

Let Go of Old Images

❧

Letting go is a vital part of the aging process. When you are able to let go of comparing yourself to when you were younger or to other young people, you are able to accept the aging process. Let go of the old images that you hold of yourself, your friends, and loved ones. By holding onto old images, you make life difficult because you are, in a sense, resisting living in the present. You are living in the past. Letting go will happen if you allow yourself to go through the emotions of aging, as we just discussed. When you experience your emotions completely, not denying nor repressing them, you will be supporting yourself in the letting go process.

It can be incredibly hard to let go of old images, especially if you saw yourself as beautiful, athletic, sexy, agile, quick-witted, or strong. The image that you now see in the mirror each morning has to change to match the reality of your present state of being. If you can redefine your self-image in a way that honors your age, you can still be sexy, beautiful, handsome, or athletic. You can then maintain the healthy self-image of your younger years. You may be surprised how powerful just adding the phrase, "for my age," can be when making positive statements about yourself. It allows you to delight in your current abilities and qualities. "I am a strong tennis player, for my age."

In addition to noticing aging in our bodies, we may notice changes in our mental capacities. Though you may know people in their 70's, 80's, and 90's who are as mentally alert now as they were when they were younger, you may notice your memory fading or your quickness of thought slowing down. To keep a strong self-image if this is happening to you, say to yourself: "I am quick-witted, for my age." Once you lose the confidence in yourself, your physical or mental capacities will continue to atrophy because, very simply, you will no longer believe in yourself and those capacities. There have been many studies done on the power of our minds. In the words of Henry Ford, "Whether you believe you can, or believe you can't, you're right!" Your reality is your perception at any given instant. Believe in yourself while at the same time letting go of old images of how you once were.

A friend of mine, Joe, found it very hard to see his ability at sports diminish with age. He was still an excellent player in his category. But he was losing to younger players whom he used to beat in the past. He also started injuring his feet, ankles, and back by trying to outplay these younger opponents. He was struggling because he kept seeing himself as someone he was twenty-five or thirty years ago, not who he was today. He had not let go of the old image of himself, and he was paying for it with injuries. Finally, one injury was severe enough that he had to be off his feet for a couple of months. This was the reflection time he needed to readjust his view of himself and update it to become current. Now he's back playing tennis and golf, but also taking on opponents who match him, and he's enjoying the competition more.

It is important to also let go of the old images you have of your friends and loved ones. Your peers are also aging. Don't expect your wife or husband to be the firm hunk or beauty she or he was 20 or 30 years ago. To hold them up to that kind of image can only cause heartache. Can you see their internal beauty? That is the important aspect to keep noticing. At the same time, you've got to change your image of your children, if you have them. Once children have left home, create new adult relation-ships with them, if you haven't already done that. If you don't

"Character makes flesh and blood comely and alive; it adorns wrinkles and old hair."
—Yehudi Menuhin

Let Go of Old Images   83

treat your children like adults, you most likely will be losing a very wonderful and meaningful part of growing older, enjoying your children as special adult friends.

Letting go of old images is a key to accepting aging. When you are able to let go of past ideas of how you (or someone else) once were, you are releasing yourself to find the joy in the moment—to feel the freedom of being ageless.

Letting Go of Old Images Exercise:

- Write down all the adjectives that described you in the past. Now look over the list. Can you say that you are still _____ (fill in the blank) "for your age"?
- What images do you have of your partner, spouse, friends, colleagues, and children? Make a list of those adjectives as well. Have you been expecting your partner to live up to a quality that is not realistic for his or her age?
- Have you let go of treating your kids as children and have you cultivated adult friendships with them?

Strategies to Jump-start Solutions:

- If you find that you are having a hard time letting go of old images and have been hard on yourself, believing you're not as good as before, then take the adjectives you wrote above and one at a time repeat to yourself: "I am _____ (fill in the blank), for my age!" Do this as often as needed to begin believing in your good qualities again.

- If you find you are hard on your spouse, partner, or peers, then similarly begin to realize they are just as good, or just as _____ (fill in the blank) "for their age."
- If you haven't begun to have adult relationships with your children (or other younger people in your life), then begin now by having a heart-to-heart talk with them. Ask them for their honest answers (and take what they say without becoming defensive). Talk about what they need from you to begin a mutually respectful relationship. Work on giving them what they need to nurture the new relationship.

Final Thoughts

When you find yourself comparing the past to the present, let go of the old images that you have of yourself and others, and this will free you to enjoy the aging process. Enjoy your memories and remember that whatever characteristics described you (or others) before, they are most likely still true today. You'll feel ageless when you accept yourself, your family, and friends as they are *now*.

"It is one thing to see your road, another to travel it."
—Anonymous

*Welcome the Wisdom
and
Gifts of Aging*

TWELVE

Make a Commitment to Yourself

❧

Commitments are important in all parts of life. In order for anything to be accomplished, there must be a commitment to make it happen. Yet there are different levels of commitment. For example, if your life depended on taking a certain medicine, you'd take it with a strong commitment, assuming you wanted to live. But we make different types of commitments depending on how concerned we are about the results. For example, some people recycle their paper, plastic, and glass because they know it's the right thing to do, but they aren't committed deeply to it. If they throw out a can or bottle here and there, it doesn't matter to them because there is only a superficial level of commitment. Some people, on the other hand, are so concerned about our environment and so passionate about taking care of the Earth that they recycle religiously.

They do *everything* in their power to recycle everywhere they are. Yes, of course, you're committed to successfully aging; that's why you bought this book. But *how* committed are you? That is the question.

How committed are you to growing and "becoming"—not just aging? Those two aspects are the secrets of being ageless—growing mentally, emotionally, and spiritually and becoming the best person you can be at this time in your life.

Make a whole-hearted commitment to this process of agelessness because the commitment is what will support you in getting the results you want. Whole-hearted means being honest about yourself and who you are now—especially about your attitudes about yourself and aging. If you lie to yourself or deny the way you really view the world and yourself, this book will be of no help.

The key here is your commitment to change—your commitment to aging in a way that makes your life more joyous, more serene, and more alive. You can have that as you age, if you are committed to it.

When you make a commitment to anything, I believe two things occur: First, you'll find a roadblock, a barrier that will present itself. If you are deeply committed, you will overcome that barrier. If you are not, the barrier will stop your forward movement. The second occurs once you pass the hurdle. You will notice that doors will open. You will find support where you hadn't noticed it before.

Years ago, after being hospitalized for an emergency appendectomy and eating nothing but bland chicken soup for my meals, I made a commitment to go home and eat low-fat and no-fat foods because of my high cholesterol. I arrived home and all my friends had gotten together to bring me meals. Guess what my first meal was? Filet mignon, topped with béarnaise sauce. (For those who don't know, béarnaise sauce is almost pure butter.) My friends, who were so loving, didn't know I had made that promise to myself. Here was my barrier. How committed was I? Did I *really* want to lower my cholesterol? Well, of course, I did, but was I *deeply* committed? No, at that time I wasn't. I ate the meal, and it has taken me years to finally be able to give up high-fat foods.

A few years later, I made a commitment to a new career by writing down a career mission statement. I was so determined to find my way in the new career that I can't even remember the barriers that were there, but I do remember the doors that opened: I met a woman who hired me as her assistant. She was an entrepreneur. I learned through osmosis how to be an

"Life is a great big canvas, and you should throw all the paint on it you can."
—Danny Kaye

entrepreneur. I also found out about classes to take, and from there learned about a valuable association to join. Doors kept opening because I had made it clear to the world and to myself that I was deeply committed.

What is your level of commitment to becoming ageless? You can make a decision about that *right now*. Or you can wait and see what you do with all the information in this book, after you've finished reading it. This book will give you ideas and choices about what kind of elder you want to be. However, ultimately it's a decision only *you* can make. If you want to achieve agelessness, you must make a *serious* commitment to doing so.

Making a Commitment to Yourself Exercise:

- Think about some of the commitments you've made in your past, both deep commitments as well as more superficial ones. What barriers presented themselves? What doors opened (including support from others)?
- What are you *deeply* committed to now? Make a list, then make another list of those things you are less committed to.
- Into which category does ageless aging fall?

Strategies to Jump-start Solutions:

- If you have a difficult time thinking about your commitments,

"*To accomplish great things, we must live as if we're never going to die.*"
—Luc de Clapiers

substitute your goals or plans (as well as adding those people and things that matter most to you).

- If you are not deeply committed to becoming ageless, you
  might consider the consequences. Take some time to look
  around you and notice those elders who are enjoying their
  lives. Notice those who aren't. Talk to them and learn what
  makes the difference in their attitudes. Whether consciously
  or not, those who are enjoying their lives are committed to
  doing so.
- When you are able to look at past commitments and notice
  the barriers and the opened doors, it will help you recognize them in the future. If you can't think of what obstacles
  or support you had with past goals or plans, ask someone
  close to you—in your personal or professional life (depending on the goal/commitment)—to remind you of what they
  may have been.

Final Thoughts

Making a deep commitment to growing mentally, emotionally,
and spiritually and becoming the best person you can be now is
important—even vital—in order to be ageless. That means not
allowing barriers to stop you from making proactive choices
for positive change. It may mean changing your attitude about
what is possible. Making a commitment also means learning to
enjoy who you are now.

THIRTEEN

"Up" Your Attitude: Be Wonder-full and Awe-some

❧

One of the most powerful tools to carry with you as you age is an up attitude. Ask people about their success and they will tell you that they had to have a positive attitude about their goals. Otherwise they would have given up and not been able to succeed.

Of course, a positive attitude means looking at the bright side of anything: "What is the silver lining here? What is the gift or the learning that I can receive here?" When you have that kind of outlook on your life, even painful moments or events will eventually bring a sense of clarity and peace simply because you have the attitude that promotes that end result.

There is more to attitude, however, and that is having the perspective of awe and wonder. So many people today, no matter what their ages, have lost their awesome-ness and their wonderfull-ness. I'm not saying that they aren't great people who aren't kind and nice. I am using these words in their figurative sense, which actually is also their basic literal sense as well. When you look at life with awe or with wonder, there are *no expectations* about how something should be. *It is expectations, I believe, that are one of the biggest destroyers of happiness in our world today.* We set about having a goal, which is a good thing. We put in the hard work that we need for the desired result to be achieved. But then we set ourselves up for disappointment because we expect the result will be *exactly* like we think it should be. We lose sight of the fact that everything in our world has variables involved. Other people and outside circumstances (such as the weather, for example) are involved. Yet we let ourselves get disappointed when something doesn't turn out as we had planned and we hold onto that dismal feeling rather than moving on. If we instead adopt an attitude of wonder and awe, we eliminate a lot of our disappointment, anger, and hurt.

Next time you have a project, goal, or plan that you are working on, instead of deciding that the result must be a certain

"The greater part of happiness depends on our dispositions and not our circumstances."
—Martha Washington

way, *wonder* what it will be. Be in awe of it, whatever the outcome. When you can go into every aspect of your life, every event, project, interaction, or goal, with an attitude of wonder or awe, you will be much happier with the result. With that simple change of perspective, you will ease your stress greatly. You will truly be awe-some and full of wonder.

When I worked for a seminar company, I traveled all over the U.S. presenting keynotes and breakout sessions at conferences. The schedules were grueling. I left home on a Sunday. Monday morning I would be dressed and ready to go at 7 A.M. I would meet the others who would be participating with me and we'd begin to set up. For 5 days in a row, we would be in a different city each day, putting in 14-hour days, presenting to crowds usually in the hundreds.

Each morning we would come into the meeting room early, usually to find that it wasn't set up as it was supposed to be. I could have let this upset me because it added to an already strenuous day. Instead, I would wake up and ask myself, "Well, I *wonder* what today's surprises will be?" By simply shifting my attitude to wonder, rather than dread, it made my life a lot happier under the circumstances.

"Life is so constructed, that the event does not, cannot, will not, match the expectation."
—Charlotte Bronte

Along these lines, keeping a positive attitude means looking at your own life only, not comparing it to someone else's. When you start comparing where John Doe was at your age, or where is he now compared with where you are, it is easy to get disappointed and sour. Keep your positive focus on your life only, without expecting outcomes and without comparing to others. When you do this, you will have discovered an important key to being ageless.

Being Wonder-full and Awe-some Attitude Exercise:

- What is your A.Q. (Attitude Quotient)? In other words, how do you look at the events in your life? Since people often fool themselves, saying they are positive thinkers when they aren't, give yourself some examples that prove you focused on the positive when things didn't turn out as you had wanted. What gifts or lessons did you learn in those circumstances? Ask five people who know you well whether they believe you have a positive attitude. Believe them!
- What kind of expectations do you *usually* have of projects, goals, and plans with which you're involved?
- What kind of expectations do you have of yourself and others? Do you expect perfection?
- Do you find yourself comparing your life with others? How does this make you feel?

Strategies to Jump-start Solutions:

- If you feel that you aren't one who focuses on the positive, start reading motivational books. Read Chapter 19 on gratitude and do the suggested strategies there. Every time you catch yourself saying or thinking something negative, stop in mid-sentence and try to restate the sentence focusing on the positive. (This does not mean you should overlook work that is not up to professional standards. Of course, if something needs to be redone, then it is important. But first, before noticing what doesn't work, notice what does.)

- Next time you are going into a situation where you find yourself expecting certain outcomes, stop and write them down. Then throw the piece of paper away. Once you have put in your time and energy into something, instead of deciding that this *must* end up in a certain way, say to yourself, "Well, I wonder what the outcome will be here?" Or, if you face daily challenges, ask yourself, "What will today's *surprises* will be?" instead of "What are today's problems going to be?"

- When you continually set your expectations too high, you will constantly be disappointed in the results. You are unhappy with yourself and others because you are judging them by standards that are unrealistic. The next time you set a standard for yourself or someone else, ask yourself, "Is this realistic?" "Could a normal, competent person really do this in the time that I have set?" If you still believe it is appropriate, ask for another person's input, someone that you trust and admire. Then consider her or his views.

♦ If you are one who compares your life with others, stop. If you can't stop immediately, then instead of comparing your life to someone who has achieved more and feeling badly, think about those who have so much less than you, and be grateful for how much you do have.

Final Thoughts

There is a saying that goes, "Your attitude determines your altitude." How high can you go with your present attitude? Your perception is your reality, and if you have a poor attitude and believe that life is awful, you will not find joy and peace as you age. Notice what works in your life (versus what doesn't work). Set goals and be in wonder or in awe at the outcome, instead of having to have it *your* way. Focus only on your own life, without comparing it to someone else's. When you have these attitudes you will certainly be able to become ageless.

"The real trick is to stay alive as long as you live."
—Ann Landers

FOURTEEN

Create Winning Decisions

❧

When you have considered several possibilities and you're about to make a choice, make it a winning decision. Look at each choice and decide what you can win or learn from each one. By believing that every decision is taking you down a successful path, you are already starting out in the right direction.

Once you make a choice, live with it. Don't play the game of "I wish I had…" You can live with regrets *or* you can believe that you made the best decision possible at the time. (You did!) That's another choice you make: What mind-set will you take with you now and after your decision has been made? Make a commitment to flourish on the path you have chosen. Realize that if you are unhappy with your choice, *after* you have given yourself a fair amount of time to try it out, you can always make another choice later on. Most of us are so fearful that we're going to make the wrong choice we stop ourselves from moving forward. We spend a lot of time worrying about our final decision, which only causes additional stress. While it's important to think through your possibilities, it's also essential to take the step and be courageous enough to live with the outcome.

When you make a decision and look back, wondering "if only...", you end up living a life full of remorse. When you continue to feel regret, you find yourself being resentful of other people, circumstances, etc. You could end up bitter about the choices you've made. Again, this is up to you. How do you want to live your life? With remorse, resentment, and bitterness? Or with joy, power, and peace of mind? You control your life by how you make and then live with your decisions.

Though it may seem simple, it can be difficult for some people to put this into practice. All it takes, however, is a change of mind to start making positive decisions. You need to believe: "I *can* win from whatever decision I make. I can learn, grow, and develop myself (my career, etc.) on whichever path I take." With that kind of thought process, your life then changes to become one of more understanding, growth, and peace of mind, if not more joy. Decide to live without regrets and

"The Excursion is the same whether you go looking for your sorrow or looking for your joy."
—Eudora Welty

believe you made the best decision you could have made at the time. From there, you move on.

Sometimes we have regret because we blame others for not giving us the promotion, down-sizing us out of a job, not saying "yes" to marrying us, or not allowing us to have another child. We can easily blame others or outside circumstances for all of our problems, if we want. This actually gives others power over us. We feel sorry for ourselves and feel helpless. It's normal to feel temporary regret as you deal with the emotional repercussions of events not going as you wished, but when you *hold on to* the emotion, it can become harmful. Regretting where you are now because of choices you made in the past will sour your heart and ultimately your face. When you regret that you didn't do something, remember you can never out-guess what your life would have been like. Regret comes from *thinking* you know what life would have been like, "if only..." Yet, the truth is that you can't know. There would have been bumps along that path, too. Don't kid yourself. What path in life has no bumps? (If you believe there is such a path, you must come back to reality, because you are only hurting yourself by believing in that fairytale.) Everything you do, every decision you make will lead to unhappiness if you believe there exists a perfect path. We are here to learn from our mistakes and grow from them. Those are what the bumps are for...to discover new truths. If we don't learn from them, we'll keep getting the same types of bumps. They may have a different face on them or be in a different setting, but until we learn certain universal truths, the same kinds of bumps will appear in our lives.

One client, Sara, found herself regretting the marriage she recently ended. She complained that she had married the wrong person at the wrong time, believing nothing good, except her grown child, had come from it. However, as much as she wanted to move on, her anger, hurt, and regret kept her emotionally tied to her ex-husband and stopped her from moving forward with her life—both with new personal relationships and at work. The stress of the internal dialog, which continued and escalated whenever she would interact with her ex-husband, was taking its toll. She developed skin rashes and breathing problems, which worsened during and after her encounters. Her medical doctors helped control the outer conditions, but she knew there was more involved. When Sara started working with me, she wanted to look at how she could change her attitude so that the times with her ex-husband would cause less stress. She knew the negative internal dialog involving her feelings of resentment and anger toward her ex-husband were partially causing her problems. She knew that she wanted to win at the decision she had made to leave her marriage and to move on in her life. That decision—to change her perspective—helped in reducing her physical symptoms as well as in giving her greater peace of mind.

Creating Winning Decisions Exercise:

- Think of a decision that needs to be made soon. Write down all the options possible. Then write everything that can be won or learned by making each choice. Next write down what challenges will be faced with each option. (This is essentially a pros and cons list for each of your choices.) You need to know them to make the choice, just not to focus solely on them.
- Make your final decision. Write all the positives about that choice and read them twice daily. Make affirmative signs and post them where you will see them. Start paying attention to what you are learning and how you are growing from this choice. Make a journal of your growth.
- Congratulate yourself for making a winning decision. Do something to celebrate your wise choice!

Strategies to Jump-start Solutions:

- If you find yourself stuck and can't find any winning outcomes from some of your choices, talk to close friends and ask if they can help. If together you can't find any positives from one

"If we could be twice as old, we could correct all our mistakes."
—Euripides

choice, then it obviously isn't the best one. However, if you *consistently* can't find any positives for all or most of your choices, then this is where you adjust your mental outlook to a positive one. Delve deeper into the possible winnings or encouraging aspects of each choice.

- Use the brainstorming techniques found in Chapter 8 on discerning what is best, if you need more options.
- Don't forget to celebrate your decision. Celebration is a healthy way to acknowledge something new in your life!

Final Thoughts

To create winning decisions, believe in yourself and your abilities to make the best choice at any given time. Believe that you made the right or best decision. Then move on, knowing that whatever the outcome is, you will be learning and growing from the decision. When you look at your choices in this way, you will find that all decisions lead to agelessness.

"It is not the years in your life but the life in your years that count."
—Adlai Stevenson

FIFTEEN

Live Today

❧

Live today means simply that: Keep your focus on the present—not the past or the future. While this involves some points made in other chapters, there is greater depth here. This is not a new concept—pain can come from living in the past or in the future. Our culture has trained us to live focused this way; however, to be content and to have peace of mind, you must live your life in the moment.

This doesn't mean that it isn't good to reminisce. It's important to remember the wonderful times in your personal history. It is detrimental to living joyfully as you age if you consistently focus on the past, with your memories of how things were (better) back then. The same is true for living in the future. It is necessary to make plans, especially with logistical aspects of your life—planning a move, retirement, or a vacation. But living daily with thoughts of, "When this happens, then I'll be happy" leads the way to misery. As soon as x, y, or z happens, you'll find something else to want or need in order for happiness to exist.

Start living now. What can you find that is good about what is happening in your life today? What needs to be changed? Do something about it; don't just wish it were otherwise. Focus on whatever you are doing at this very moment. In this case, you're reading this book; take it in, think about it, but don't let yourself get distracted by the cleaning, the doctor's appointment, or something else. Just be here, in the moment, reading this book.

With any and everything that you do on a daily basis, be focused on it. Avoid being distracted by worries, the to-do list, or anything else. When you find yourself concentrating on the task at hand, rather than daydreaming in other directions, you'll find more peace of mind and joy in *whatever* you are doing.

Of course, it's easy to focus on momentary tasks or activities that already bring contentment, whether it's sewing, reading, swimming, or golfing. But this also works for the more mundane aspects of life, too. If there are tasks at work or at

"A long life may not be good enough, but a good life is long enough."
—Benjamin Franklin

home that are boring, when you pay attention to them *in the moment*—without wishing you were doing something else—they will become less annoying.

Try this with a chore you dislike. (You may want to come back to this activity after you read Chapter 17 on eliminating what you don't like.) When you find that you must do something that you don't like, eliminate all other thoughts from your head as you do it. Concentrate completely on the task at hand.

I learned this concept years ago and decided to try it on one of my most disliked chores—cleaning the house. I took the mop; focused on it as I squeezed the excess moisture from it. I looked intently at the area on the floor that I was mopping, noticing inch by inch what specks were there and watching how I wiped them clean. I heard the swish of the mop. I felt the handle gripped in my fingers and noticed the textures of the handle, the mop, and the floor. If you can be in the moment as intently as I've just described, I believe two things will happen: (a) The chore will go more quickly because you won't be wishing yourself to be elsewhere and your concentration will move you along, and (b) You will find the chore not only more enjoyable, because again you won't be *comparing* it to what you could have been doing, but you will also find it meditative. It can be soothing to your mind because you are eliminating all other thoughts. (This is one of the goals of meditation—to eliminate the junk or clutter from your mind.)

Living in the moment creates a state of peace even when the moment is a distressful one. If you are feeling angry or fearful, allow yourself to feel that way. Don't repress it, pretending that you can handle it. Of course you can handle it, *and* you can be angry or afraid at the same time. To be in the moment with your emotions is important because, as mentioned before, you will be able to move through those emotions more easily by being *in* them, rather than trying to get *out of* them.

If you wish to be ageless, begin now to take each moment as it comes, to live in the present. When you are only experiencing where you are now, what you are doing now, and not thinking about what was before, what could have been, or what might be in the future, you will find a great sense of peace.

Whenever you start feeling agitated about what is going on, ask yourself, "Am I experiencing this moment, or am I wishing something were different?" Remember the old expression, "We are human be-ings, not human do-ings." If you want to live as a human be-ing, be and live today.

Living Today Exercise:

- How much time do you spend thinking or daydreaming about the past, what could have been, or how things were back then?
- How much time do you spend thinking or worrying about the future, where you need to be, how much has to be completed in such a short amount of time, what you wish you were doing instead, or what will happen next?
- Have you ever tried to live completely in the moment, with your chores or other unpleasant tasks as in the mopping example mentioned earlier? Do you believe it's possible to feel at peace doing something you don't like?

Strategies to Jump-start Solutions:

- If you don't have any idea about the amount of time you spend either in the future or in the past, try this: Get a sheet of paper. Make three columns, labeled "Past," "Present," and "Future." Set your watch or a timer for every 10 or 15 minutes. When the beeper goes off, notice exactly what was on your mind in those seconds or minutes before it went off. Make tally marks under one of the three categories. You will then have a clearer idea about what your mind is doing.
- If you have never tried something like the mopping example, it would be a wonderful experiment to try. However, be *open*

> "Be mindful of how you approach time. Watching the clock is not the same as watching the sunrise."
>
> —Anonymous

to the possibility that a disagreeable chore *could* be meditative or calming when done in this manner. If you have already made up your mind that it won't work, then there is no point in trying this because you have pre-judged the outcome.

Final Thoughts

Whenever you live in the present moment, you will find that life is more enjoyable. You aren't comparing this moment to some past situation nor to a future that is only a daydream. You are experiencing everything as it is *now*. There is peace, joy, and grace in each moment, if you are open to it. Allow yourself to live today, to be in the moment, as a core element of being ageless.

SIXTEEN

Distill the Essence of Your Joys

I have heard from numerous elders who said that "Life isn't wonderful anymore. I used to be able to do this or that, and now because of my heart condition (or other infirmity), I can't do that any more." When this loss first occurs, it's understandable to feel grief, anger, shame, and/or resentment. If you stay mired in those emotions, however, you are stopping yourself from finding new joy in your life as it is now. While there are people who ski, hike, or jog into their nineties, the majority of people, when they get older, give up activities or slow down in areas they excelled in before.

Sometimes our knees just give out or literally get ground down from wear and tear. This is part of honoring your body and its timing. So what can you do? Give up, resign, and believe that life has nothing to offer you because you can't do a certain activity anymore? That's not being ageless! To age successfully, you've still got to put joy into your life, in whatever way you can. So how do you do this?

You do it by finding the *essence* of your joys. Let's say as a younger man, you loved to play football. But you can't do that any more. You distill the essence of that joy by asking yourself, *"What exactly was it about playing football that I loved so much?* Was it the team sports aspect? The camaraderie? The fans cheering me on the sidelines? Being on stage, so to speak? Was it the game itself? Did I love the tactical aspect of it? Was it running down a field? Was it simply being outside on a cold crisp autumn day? Think about *every* aspect that you loved about it and then find another way to bring those aspects of football into your life now.

Let's take another example. Say as a young woman, you loved ballet dancing. *What exactly was it about ballet that you loved?* The hard training? The stretching and making your body do things that you didn't think it could do? The classical music being played on the piano as accompaniment? Dancing to music, no matter what the steps were? Dressing up in costume? Putting on recitals? Make a list of each component that was part of your joy in doing that activity. The list contains the ingredients or the essence of your joys.

Once you distill the essence of your joys, then you need to find ways to bring the same essence into your life now. For example, if you loved the teamwork aspect of football, then find a way to be on a different kind of a team. Are there golf tournaments that you can play on in teams? Or, buy some board games and get a bunch of friends together and play in teams? If it was being cheered, or being on stage, what about joining a local theater group? If you loved the classical music as a ballerina, make sure you play plenty of classical music in your home. If you loved the pure dancing, then either find ways to bring dance into your life—take a ballroom or ethnic dance class, or put on music and dance around your own living room. If it was dressing up in costume, have some costume parties. Be creative in figuring out new ways to bring into your life the essence of your joys.

I love to travel; it's a deep passion of mine. One of my favorite activities—one of the essences of my passion for travel—is driving the back roads and smaller highways in Europe, seeing the open vistas, the natural scenery, and visiting the quaint towns along the way. When work keeps me here, in California, I give myself this essence by driving the back roads of the surrounding counties where I live. No, it's not Europe, but it gives me great pleasure nonetheless.

A friend of mine fell in love with having high tea in Victoria, British Columbia. There was such elegance, decadence, and regal atmosphere to it that she felt completely pampered. When she got home from her trip, she dusted off all her old china and gave herself a tea party; she hired her teenage daughter and a friend to serve and was able to have the same kind of experience that she enjoyed in Victoria.

A client applied this process to her love of needlepoint. Her arthritic hands were finding it harder and harder to work with the tiny stitches. When she found the essences of this joy, she realized it was solitude, attention to detail, and appreciation of beauty that she loved so much before. She became involved in ikebana—the Japanese art of flower arranging. She was still able to work in solitude and enjoy the beauty of her creations, and it was much less painful to her fingers.

Some people put themselves in binds when they say to themselves, "Well, if I can't have it the way it was before, then I won't be able to have it at all." If you wish to age with happiness, to become ageless, then distill the essence of your joys and bring that essence into your life in as many ways as possible.

Distilling the Essence of Your Joys Exercise:
- What were your joys from long ago (childhood, as a teenager, young adulthood) that you no longer do now?
- What have you had to give up due to physical, mental, or financial reasons?
- Take the lists from above and, with each item, find the essence of your joys: With each joy, ask yourself, *"What is it exactly that I love about _____?"* List these elements or the essences of each activity.
- With each essence, brainstorm different ways you can bring that element into your life again in a way that is compatible with your current lifestyle.

Strategies to Jump-start Solutions:
- If you have trouble remembering back, ask your siblings, parents, or long-time friends about what you loved when you were younger.
- If you are able to do everything you love and haven't given anything up due to health reasons, keep up the good work. Now you'll know what to do in case physical or financial changes create the need to alter your lifestyle.

"As you grow older, you'll find the only things you regret are the things you didn't do."
—Zachary Scott

- If you are having trouble distilling the essence of your joys, bring friends or loved ones into this conversation also. Have them help brainstorm the different possibilities that may be the essences of each joy, as well as different ways to bring this joy into your life in a new way.

Final Thoughts

Life at any age and any stage can be full of vitality, passion, and excitement when you find pleasure in it. When you bring back the essence of your joys into your life, your life will be filled with more happiness. Saying this new way isn't the same as it was before, and *equating* that with it being less good, can cause you discontent. Instead, enjoy the new essence as something different and exciting, and at the same time, remember that your deepest desires, the essence of your joys, are being achieved.

SEVENTEEN

Eliminate What You Don't Like and Can't Change

❧

After you distill the essence of your joys, the second half of finding more happiness as you age is to eliminate what you don't like in your life and can't change. What are those things, big and little, which are difficult to live with? What things can you change? Be honest here because we often can change things but are too afraid to try and make the effort or to confront a person whose behavior is difficult for us to be around. We can make those changes, but we have to be assertive to make them. Don't eliminate this step if you want to find joy as you age. You will have to be assertive about your desires.

If you have tried to make changes and can't, or if you have been assertive about behaviors that you don't like but have found a resistant person, then it's time to find out other ways to deal with this concern. What needs to be eliminated in order to feel joy?

Many people live a resigned life. They feel reconciled to doing activities that may not hurt them but may give them little or no pleasure. They live with little irritants that they feel resigned to have in their lives, and they assume they will always have to live with them. For example, chores can be those kinds of irritants or stressors; those things that must be done but which you hate doing. It doesn't kill you to clean the bathroom, but you end up resentful every time you do it. Or you may hate it that *you* are the one who always takes out the garbage. Of course, you can do it, but you'd rather work in the garden or wash dishes. There are things you've lived with for years because you have always thought that they had to be done, and you've always believed that you were the one who had to do them. There are ways, however, to eliminate these kinds of chores or to make changes, *if* you are willing to accept the alternatives.

If you don't like cleaning house, why are you doing it? Yes, you value a clean house, but here are two questions to ask yourself: First, are you a perfectionist and are your standards such that you have to clean it all the time? In other words, if you only cleaned a few hours once a week instead of daily picking up, would you be happier? Can you accept the alternative of a house that isn't spotlessly clean all the time? Secondly, who says *you* have to do it? Have you enlisted the help of your spouse or partner and/or your live-at-home children? Have you given them the responsibility to clean it, too? What if you live alone and you can't find anyone to share the responsibility? Can you trade with a friend? Trading is an excellent way to eliminate what you don't like and can't change.

Lastly, look at your budget. If you hate cleaning so much, can you eliminate something else in your budget (like shopping for new clothes as often as you shop now or your daily mocha) and budget in a cleaning person instead? There are creative ways to eliminate what you don't like, if you are willing to spend the time necessary to work it out. The payoff is great, however. You will feel more joy when you eliminate those things you dislike.

We get stuck in the chores of life, thinking there are no alternatives, but the truth is that there are usually more choices and more answers to problems than we believe. If you are one who sees this issue of eliminating what you don't like, as black or white, then go back to the chapter on discernment (Chapter 8) and do the activities on brainstorming. As with everything, be willing to change your perspective about your choices.

"If you don't risk anything, you risk even more."
—Erica Jong

If you believe that all the alternatives are disagreeable, you will be angry or resentful no matter what. It will be your choice to view each possible solution in that way. You will not, however, find yourself living with much joy in your life because of the mind-set that you have chosen. If you can find one or more possible solutions that work better than the others and you have a positive attitude, you will be on the right track to living with more joy and contentment.

When all else fails and you cannot change or eliminate those things you dislike, you can at least change your perspective about the activity itself. One way to help do this is to re-read the chapter on "Live Today." If you use the technique of focusing completely on what you are doing, even unpleasant chores seem less difficult.

In a workshop that I presented in Belgium, when we did the activities about brainstorming new ways to eliminate or change the unwanted chores in life, two women who were friends decided to exchange duties. One hated house cleaning; the other hated grocery shopping. They worked out a plan where each would do the disagreeable chore for the other. They were so surprised that there was such an easy solution to something they had grumbled about for years. I hate reconciling my bank statements, so I have arranged my budget to accommodate a bookkeeper, rather than get frustrated on a regular basis. In the past, I have traded my coaching services for house cleaning. You can find solutions to common irritants if you exercise your creativity, enlist the help of others, and/or change your perspective.

Eliminating What You Don't Like Exercise:

- What are you doing in your life right now, on a regular basis, that you really dislike doing? Make two lists, one of the really distasteful activities or irritants, and the other of chores/irritants that you don't like, but that aren't threatening to your overall sense of happiness.
- Go back to the lists mentioned above. Think about what you've already done to try and change them. Be honest. Have you seriously tried to make changes or just *resigned* yourself to living with the way things are?
- What can you do to change or eliminate those activities or issues that are real irritants? Be creative with your answers.
- Which of these activities needs an attitude readjustment, such as focusing on it in the moment or letting go of it completely?

Strategies to Jump-start Solutions:

- If you don't have any irritating chores or activities in your

"Live all you can; it's a mistake not to."
—Henry James

life, congratulate yourself! Either you're one step ahead of most people, or you aren't being honest with yourself.

- ◆ Use brainstorming techniques discussed in Chapter 8 to help come up with ways to change or eliminate those things you dislike. Involve family and/or friends who might be interested in doing some creative trading.
- ◆ If you find that you think you need to do everything yourself if it's going to be done well, be willing to live without perfection. Perfectionism causes unnecessary stress in your life and usually is accompanied by resentment, anger, or frustration.

Final Thoughts

You can eliminate those things you dislike if you are willing to make the effort to create some changes in the way you do things now. Four key ideas here are:

1. Trading chores or activities,
2. Reallocating resources to fund what is causing you great stress or unhappiness,
3. Letting go of some of your perfectionism to free up time to do something more important, and/or
4. Changing your perspective about the activity itself.

When you are able to spend less time on those annoying chores, you will find yourself living with more joy and peace of mind.

"It is not our job to work miracles, but it is our task to try."
—Joan Chittister

EIGHTEEN

Stay Lovingly and Compassionately Connected

Staying lovingly and compassionately connected is vital to aging well. It is important to give and receive love, no matter what our age. Staying involved with friends, family, colleagues, and even pets is important. Chemicals released from our emotions are in every one of our cells according to research done in the early '90s. When loving emotions are present, we generally feel happier and more content with life (and heal faster from illnesses). Much research has been done on the importance of loving connections and healing faster.

You may be wondering what it means to have loving connections. It means simply that you *aim* to love unconditionally. Most of us don't do this well. This is often easier to do with pets than with friends or family members. (After all, pets don't talk back, and they will eventually do what you want them to if they want to get fed!) Can you love a person even while feeling angry or being afraid of him or her? Can you love people even if they don't fulfill your expectations? Loving and feeling compassion for people is accepting them, as they are now, whether or not they ever change, do what you want them to do, or behave in any particular way. You don't have to condone or go along with their beliefs, behaviors, or ideas, but you feel love and compassion for them as they are now. When you feel compassion you believe that whomever you are dealing with is doing the best that they can at this moment. If they are behaving in ways you don't like, compassion means giving them understanding and realizing life must be hard for them to behave the way that they are. This is why loving unconditionally is so challenging.

Many of us have been taught conditional love by our parents, our religion, and our culture. The unspoken message was, "I'll love you *if*..." While they may have really loved us, even if we didn't do what they wanted, their actions were what we believed. (Today's parents seem to be better at expressing displeasure at behavior and still holding love for their children when they say: "I love you *and* I don't like the way you are behaving.")

Staying lovingly connected is what is needed in the emotional realm for a sense of well-being in all of life, not only as we age. With all the options for staying connected today (in person, via phone, Internet, and with social, political, and other nonprofit organizations), there is virtually no excuse for not finding a way to stay connected with people. If it is difficult to stay connected with people due to physical and financial limitations, consider pets. They can help you stay lovingly connected, too. The loving relationships you develop are what help you access your compassion.

> *"For those who grow old, life is at its sweetest."*
> —Sophocles

The more people in your life who you can give love to and receive love from, the more enriched your life will be. Except for a few people who are true hermits or loners, most people need the camaraderie and support of others. At the same time, we all have our differences in how much time we need in solitude and with people. The more we can have that feeling of love and compassion, the more we will be able to receive it back. Opening your heart instead of closing it will reap rewards that will help you feel ageless.

A friend of mine, Lori, was transferred to a new city with her job. She was single, an introvert, and had two sisters living back home. Though she met people at work, it was a challenge for her to connect socially and she felt isolated. It was causing her anxiety, sadness, and loneliness. After realizing the importance of staying lovingly connected, she initiated even more contact with her sisters, started asking women at work to meet her for drinks in the evenings, and found groups who did volunteer work for local charities that matched her interests. While it was difficult to take the leap to initiate the contacts, she later was delighted that she had. The connections gave her life new meaning and eliminated her loneliness.

Staying Lovingly Connected Exercise:
- How are you staying lovingly connected with family, friends, colleagues, and/or pets?
- Who and what do you love unconditionally? Who or what else do you want to add to this list?
- Who or what do you feel deep, satisfying love from?
- When was the last time you openly expressed your feelings to those you love? When was the last time they expressed love toward you?
- Make a list of what can you do to increase the ways you stay lovingly and compassionately connected.

Strategies to Jump-start Solutions:
- If you are having a difficult time staying lovingly connected

"Only friends will tell you the truths you need to hear to make ...your life bearable."
—Francine du Plessix Gray

with people in your life, ask yourself why? Think about what you can do to improve this. If you don't have family living nearby, then concentrate on friends. If you are restricted in your ability to go out and socialize, stay connected via phone, email, and/or ask people to come visit you, even if it is a service or volunteer organization, such as Council on Aging. Stay connected by adopting a pet from the pound. If you are allergic to cats and dogs, try a bird or an aquarium of fish. Volunteer in schools, with Big Brothers and Sisters, or in any nonprofit agency that deals directly with people.

◆ If you feel your list is too short (of either those whom you feel love for or those whom you want to feel love from), think about friends and family members you would like to add. Do something to show your care for them *today*—write or email them a short note, give them a call, visit them, or bring/send a small gift. Tell them how much you care.

◆ If you don't feel unconditional love, what can you ask for in your relationships that will help you feel more love and acceptance?

◆ If it has been a long time since you have been in touch with these family members and friends, don't stop after reaching out just once. Make sure you keep in contact with them *regularly*. It may take them a while to recognize your sincere desire to reconnect.

- Start now and follow through on the ways you can stay connected. Don't use excuses to keep you from adding this important component of joy to your life.

Final Thoughts

The benefits you reap from staying lovingly connected will far outweigh the effort it takes. They will also outweigh the embarrassment or shame that you might feel if it has been a long time since you've reached out to these friends or family members. When I have talked to elders who have done this, the overwhelming response has been, "I wish I had done this sooner." Sharing more love and compassion for all those around you will fill your heart with joy, increasing the contentment you feel as you age.

NINETEEN

Be Grateful for the Little Moments

❧

One cause of regret or bitterness later in life is that people often think they should have acquired this, achieved that, or done something they hadn't done. They think they should have had this promotion, visited these many places, or had this much money. We, as Americans, seem to always want *more*. In that process, which is so much about living in the past and the future rather than in the present, we have lost sight of what we have *now*. We often think it is the big material gains in our lives that bring us joy and those are what we remember to be thankful for.

In the meantime, we forget to be thankful for everything as it is at this very moment. When you are grateful for all that you have, there is a great sense of contentment that wells up within.

You know there are treasures right in front of you and you appreciate them. Look in the mirror and look at the treasure that you are—your wisdom from all the experiences of your lifetime. Look around you and notice all that you have, in personal possessions as well as in relationships, and be grateful for them. Try to stop wanting. Meditate on all the wonder that is in your life right now.

Realize that the little moments in life are what really count in life. They add up to the big results. A beautiful sunny day is something to be grateful for. If your child or grandchild gave you a smile or a hug, be grateful. If you are reading a good book, be grateful that you can read and that you have something fascinating in front of you. When you are talking to a friend on the phone, be grateful for that connection. There are so many people, sights, sounds, and events in daily life to be grateful for. They are the simple moments in life. When you are grateful for these little instances, you will find yourself happier and more content. Each and every one of us has so many things to be grateful for. Life's rewards are many, if you can notice them and be thankful for all that you have.

Add up all your little moments and notice how much you already have. You can want more or different. There's nothing wrong with that. Most people want more or different because they believe that what they have isn't good enough. Realize that what you already have is good; be grateful and then move toward what you want by making the changes necessary to bring about your desired results. It's important to be thankful, however, in order to feel a deep sense of contentment, rather than seeking an elusive outcome, which, in and of itself, doesn't bring rewards or satisfaction.

The first time I started paying attention to goals and dreams was right after my divorce. Up until that point, I was content to just let life happen. After discovering the power of our minds and the importance of goals, I swung to the opposite direction. I was extremely focused about making myself and my life better. I pursued my dreams with determination. I also lost the ability to be grateful for what I had. I forgot to be thankful for all the little elements in my life that were wonderful right then and there. I had expectations that I could make good things happen, and when life wasn't as good as I wanted it to be, I was disappointed or resentful.

Eventually, I got the message and remembered how awe-inspiring sunsets are, how heart-warming hugs can be, and how humbling it is to be alive and to live in this grand Universe.

> *"Life is short, and it's up to you to make it sweet."*
>
> —Sadie Delany

Now, I am grateful for many little things... even the perfect parking spot on a crowded shopping day!

Being Grateful for the Little Moments Exercise:

- When was the last time you felt full of gratitude for your life? In general, how often do you feel gratitude?
- What and who are you grateful for? Are you usually only thankful for the big things in life or are you also regularly grateful for the small moments as well?
- Do you feel happy with the way your whole life is right now? If not, what areas are you grateful for and what needs changing? What are you doing to bring about the necessary changes so that you can be grateful for all of your life?
- Even if you aren't grateful for *all* of your life, can you find some things in each area of life to be thankful for?

Strategies to Jump-start Solutions:

- If it has been a long time since you've felt gratitude, stop a moment and look around you, think about all that you have, and feel the gratitude for it all now. Then each morning or evening, stop and take a moment to be grateful.
- If you can't think of much, start a gratitude journal. Every day write three or more things that you were grateful for that day. Make sure some of them are the little moments in your life.

- If you aren't happy with your life right now, begin by going back to the first strategy and feeling gratitude for whatever you can think of right now. Then decide what you want to change. Remember, you can only change yourself and your circumstances, so writing down that you want to change your partner or your boss isn't possible. You can change the circumstances regarding your partner or boss, however. You can also change your attitude toward them, once you have decided what you want to change. Choose the most important change needing to be made and write down the steps necessary to achieve it. Then start today doing one thing that will bring that goal into reality. Each day continue to do something toward the result that you want. Remember to feel gratitude along the way.

Final Thoughts

To be ageless and have joy and peace of mind, have an attitude of gratitude. Begin now to appreciate and be grateful for *all* the small moments of goodness in your life. There is in life a "grateful cycle," just like there is a "vicious cycle." In the vicious cycle, one bad thing leads to another. In the grateful cycle one good thing, which you are thankful for, leads you to find another. Pretty soon you are noticing many wonderful things and being grateful for them all. Your mood is elevated

"Life would be infinitely happier if we could only be born at the age of 80 and gradually approach 18."
—Mark Twain

because you are becoming aware of all the good that is in your life and you are feeling the warmth and contentment of being grateful.

TWENTY

Trust— In Yourself, in Life, and in Something Bigger

❧

The things that never change in life are death and taxes, goes the old saying. But it isn't taxes that we fear (usually)—it's the unknown of our death. Hundreds of years ago, death was considered a natural part of life, like birth. Somewhere in our history, however, we've lost sight of that. Death is a part of life. We have become so scientific, so left-brained, we think we can become immortal if we can just find the cures to all diseases and replace body parts with bionic mechanisms. Yet, even if we found the cures to all existing diseases, new ones would appear. Even if we replaced body parts with the latest technological wonders, there still would be death, sooner or later. When we can accept that we will die, and understand on a deep emotional level that death is a natural part of our life, we can live with greater peace of mind, find joy in the moment, and live in grace.

What we have to do is trust—have faith in ourselves, that we are doing the very best we can be doing at any given moment, and that we have the abilities and capabilities to do whatever is necessary. We also need to trust that if we *don't* have the abilities or inner resources to do what needs to be done, at least, we know where to find help. We also need to trust in the process of life, and that means accepting our own death. Lastly, we need to have faith in Something Bigger, in a spiritual connection—whatever that may be for each of us.

Trusting in ourselves, in our capabilities, can be difficult if we don't have self-confidence. That is the basis for trusting ourselves. Yet even without confidence in ourselves, we can still trust that we can get the help or find the resources needed.

Having faith in the process of life is more difficult. All of us have a great need to control our circumstances, and we can't always do that. There are so many variables that are beyond our control. To combat this desire to control, simply do your best, put in the hard work that is necessary to achieve the desired results, and then let go of your expectations of the outcome. When you have that kind of a perspective, it makes life easier. You won't see failure as the end result; you'll see it only as one step along your path, realizing that there is another step to take right after that.

Trusting in the process of life is about accepting the fact that we will die one day. When we can understand death without fearing it, we can live our lives in joy and trust. There is an ebb and flow in life. Eventually, everything declines. You can stay more physically active if you exercise your body. For example, doing stretching, aerobics, weight training, walking, or yoga will help keep your body fit. You can stay more mentally alert if you actively stretch your brain. For example, playing games, doing puzzles, or learning *anything* new, will keep your mind exercised. You can stay more emotionally alive if you actively exercise your heart by staying lovingly connected with others. Yet, there will come a time when you won't be able to do the same things that you did before. Your body and mind will change as you get older. No matter what shape your body or mind is in, you will still die eventually.

You can live in fear of this event, or you can accept death as a natural part of your existence. While it is natural for many people to fear death, you don't have to let it rule your life.

"Nothing must be postponed; find eternity in each moment."
—Henry David Thoreau

When you let it color your whole world, it taints everything you do, think, and feel. Some people stop living long before their death because of their fear of it. They keep tight reigns and limits on their choices—not risking a new adventure because of this pervasive fear. When you accept that your death will occur and you very simply go on living and enjoying your life in the moment, there is a sense of peace that prevails within you. Trusting in the life process from birth to death can help you in living *now*, aging with joy, serenity, and confidence.

Many people have lost their complete faith in Something Bigger, or their spiritual connection. (Use the name that is best for you: God, Our Creator, Buddha, Holy Spirit, The Universe, The One, Allah, Jesus, All That Is, The Source, Mother Earth, Father Sky, Spirit, etc.) Why have they lost their trust? Growing up they became disillusioned by rules, procedures, and rituals, generating guilt, shame, or fear that damaged their belief. If you have lost your faith in Spirit, try to step out of the old paradigm that cut you off from believing. Look at Spirit in the greater sense.

Spirit is the umbrella for all religions of the world, not in opposition to any of them. As we age, it is important to remember our spiritual connection. Whether you are a member of a religious community or not, the important thing is to keep your spiritual relationship *alive*, not to put it aside as you age. When you keep your spiritual connection, whatever and however it may be, it will create contentment within you for whatever is happening in your life right now.

I went for many years without a sense of spiritual connection. I had grown up in a family with mixed religious backgrounds but without much spiritual connection and not a lot of reverence for the grandness of life. So I never had the background that could have brought me into the spiritual realm of life. I always thought that was a disadvantage, yet friends who were steeped in religious upbringing felt their indoctrination was stifling and wished they'd had the opposite upbringing. Either way, some of us may find that it's a challenge to get reconnected.

For me, it all began with a class that started opening me up to a greater spiritual connection. Then one day, I experienced the meaning and the power of Spirit like a bolt of lightning. Since that time, I have allowed myself to trust in the outcome of the events of my life. This has helped tremendously with my stress. I don't worry nearly as much (yes, I still worry!), and I usually

"Youth of the Heart, Soul and Mind is everlasting."
—Jean Paul Friedrich Richter

get to a point where I can say, "Okay, I let go...I've done my best. Now I have to wait and see the results."

Having faith in Spirit and keeping your spiritual connection alive will ease your pain, bring you peace of mind, and help you find the joy in being ageless.

Trusting Exercise:
+ How trusting do you feel about your own capabilities? How trusting are you of your ability to find help if you don't have the resources yourself?
+ Do you trust in your life's process? Do you trust that things will turn out okay, even if they aren't always what you want?
+ Can you accept your own mortality?
+ Do you feel connected spiritually? Do you trust in Spirit? How would you describe your trust and faith?

Strategies to Jump-start Solutions:
+ In what areas do you wish you felt more capable? List them and think about avenues you can explore to improve your abilities.
+ If you find yourself not trusting that everything will be okay, look back on some past events or circumstances where the outcome was less than you expected. Use these past events

"It isn't until you come to a spiritual understanding of who you are that you begin to take control."

—Oprah Winfrey

as a foundation to prove to yourself that, though the results were not what you had wanted, you lived through it (and hopefully learned something valuable as well).

- If you have a hard time accepting your own mortality, go to a senior center and talk to the elders there. Read *Tuesdays With Morrie*, by Mitch Albom, or other books and stories of people who have come face to face with their own mortality and have done so with grace.

- If you are happily involved in a religious or spiritual community, then you may want to become more active. If you have left a religion because of negative associations, spend some time finding out about the spiritual communities near you and/or read books in the Western and Eastern Religion/ Philosophy sections of your library or bookstore. Ask close friends about their affiliations and join them to see if it might be right for you. Learn to meditate and create your own unique spiritual connection.

Final Thoughts

Trusting in yourself, trusting in the process of life, and trusting in Spirit will help you tremendously to embrace your life's path. Accepting your own mortality and realizing that we all have an end to this life will grant you the serenity that is necessary to age with grace, peace of mind, and joy—to become ageless.

The End of the Beginning

❧

Now that you've read this book and done the exercises and/or used the strategies to jump-start your own solutions, I hope that you've arrived here with a better understanding of yourself and ways to become ageless.

There is a saying, "Knowledge is power." Knowledge, however, is only the foundation for true power. This, alone, will not change the way you are or the way others perceive you. This won't give you the ingredients to feel like the wise elder that you can be. The second and equally important part of acquiring the power needed to age successfully is in its application. In other words, "Just do it!" Start *proactively* making positive changes in the way you be-have and think if you are to get the most from this book. If you want to be able to age happily, begin the process without delay.

Go back to the Table of Contents and jot down a few of the chapters that meant the most to you; those ideas that had the greatest impact. Was it honoring your body and body-time or discovering the essence of your joys? Perhaps it was the reminder to trust in the process of life or take responsibility for yourself. Whatever topics grabbed you, take them *one at a time* and start constructing a new way of being. Catch yourself when you do or say something in your old way. Don't beat yourself up for slipping backwards—we all do it from time to time. Just notice it, in the moment, and then redo it, but differently this time. Go back and do what you were doing or saying in the *new* way. The way we change is to practice a new way. . . and it takes *practice, patience, and persistence*. Don't get discouraged if it's harder than you thought. Think how long it took you to get where you are now. . . so, of course, it will take time to make these changes permanent.

What is important to remember is that you've already taken the first step by reading this book. Continue to *focus only on the next step*, remembering your goals, but not spending your time worrying about whether you'll get there or not. You will get there if you use the three "p's" mentioned in the last paragraph: practice, patience, and persistence!

Begin this by taking your most important topic and making it a goal to change your thoughts and behavior to reflect this aspect of aging with joy. Write it in an affirmative statement and then write down what you imagine your feelings will be when you reach it. For example, "I feel excited and happy when I am creating winning decisions." Or, "I feel confident and proud when I assert myself." Read this statement every day, morning and night, to reinforce your motivation. Every time you make a winning decision or assert yourself, reward yourself in some small way. Do this for at least a month. Then move on to another goal.

That's how it's done—one small step at a time. Keep remembering how great you feel when you act and think in ways that allow you to age with joy, vitality, and confidence. Remember the enduring and endearing qualities that contribute to being ageless.

You can do it…I know you can!

Blessings!

Suzy Allegra

P.S. I am interested in your stories. Write and tell me how you've learned to age with joy, serenity, and vitality; with passion, power, and purpose. We can all learn from each other. I look forward to hearing of your success.

Please write to me at:

Suzy Allegra
P.O. Box 4494
Santa Rosa, CA 95402-4494 USA
Email: suzy@suzyallegra.com

About the Author

To book Suzy for a speaking or coaching engagement with your company or organization, please:

Call: 707.527.8872 or 866.JOY2AGE (toll free)

or Email: suzy@suzyallegra.com

or Write: Suzy Allegra
             P.O. Box 4494
             Santa Rosa, CA 95402-4494 USA

Visit Suzy's website at:
www.suzyallegra.com

Suggested Readings

Baron, Renee & Wagele, Elizabeth. *The Enneagram Made Easy*. San Francisco: HarperSanFrancisco, 1994

Brian, Cynthia. *Be the Star You Are: 99 Gifts for Living, Loving, Laughing, and Learning to Make a Difference*. Berkeley, CA: Ten Speed Press, 2001

Cameron, Julia. *The Artist's Way: a Spiritual Path to Higher Creativity*. Los Angeles, CA: Jeremy P. Tarcher/Perigee, 1992

Carter, Jimmy. *The Virtues of Aging*. New York: The Ballantine Publishing Group, 1998

Casey, Karen. *Keepers of the Wisdom: Reflections from Lives Well Lived*. Center City, MN: Hazelden, 1996

Chopra, Deepak, M.D. *Ageless Body, Timeless Mind: The Quantum Alternative to Growing Old*. New York: Harmony Books, 1993

Cohen, Gene D., M.D., Ph.D. *The Creative Age*. New York: HarperCollins Publishers, 2000

Dass, Ram. *Still Here: Embracing Aging, Changing, and Dying.* New York: Riverhead Books, 2001

Dychtwald, Ken, Ph.D. & Flower, Joe. *Age Wave.* New York: Bantam Books, 1990

Friedan, Betty. *The Fountain of Age.* New York: Touchstone/ Simon & Schuster, 1994

Gawain, Shakti. *Creative Visualization.* Berkeley, CA: Bantam Books, 1978

Gerike, Ann E. Ph.D. *Old is Not a Four-Letter Word.* Watsonville, CA: Papier-Mâché Press, 1997

Hendricks, Gay and Kathleen. *Conscious Loving: The Journey to Co-Commitment.* New York: Bantam Books, 1990

Huss, Sally. *The Happy Book: 30 Fun-Filled Exercises for Greater Joy.* Berkeley, CA: Ten Speed Press, 2000

Jeffers, Susan J. *Feel the Fear and Do It Anyway.* San Diego, CA: Harcourt Brace Jovanovich, 1987

Jensen, Eric. *The Little Book of Big Motivation.* New York: Fawcett Columbine, 1995

Kramp, Erin and Douglas. *Living with the End in Mind*. New York: Three Rivers Press, 1998

Louden, Jennifer. *The Woman's Comfort Book*. San Francisco, CA: HarperSanFrancisco, 1992

Maggio, Rosalie. *Quotations from Women on Life*. Paramus, NJ: Prentice Hall, 1997

McKay, Matthew, Ph.D. & Fanning, Patrick. *The Daily Relaxer*. Oakland, CA: New Harbinger Publications, 1997

Northrup, Christiane, M.D. *The Wisdom of Menopause: Creating Physical and Emotional Health and Healing During the Change*. New York: Bantam Books, 2001

Rechtschaffen, Stephan, M.D. *Timeshifting: Creating More Time to Enjoy Your Life*. New York: Doubleday, 1997

Roizen, Michael F., M.D. *RealAge*. New York: Cliff Street Books, 1999

Sark. *Living Juicy: Daily Morsels for Your Creative Soul*. Berkeley, CA: Ten Speed Press, 1993

Sher, Barbara. *Wishcraft: How to Get What You Really Want*. New York: Viking Press, 1979

Simon, Dr. Sidney B., Howe, Dr. Leland W., & Kirschenbaum, Dr. Howard. *Values Clarification.* New York: Warner Books, Inc., 1995

Stoddard, Alexandra. *Grace Notes.* New York: Avon Books, 1994

Von Oech, Roger. *A Whack on the Side of the Head.* New York: Warner Books, Inc., 1990

Weil, Andrew, M.D. *Natural Health, Natural Medicine.* Boston, MA: Houghton Mifflin Company, 1990

NOTES